This book is dedicated to
Teresa Chin
1962-2007

Embedded Comedian
Jim McCue

MATT
ALL the best!

(autograph signature)

Preface

There is a fine line between laughter and sorrow. That line grows slimmer when one is confronted with the horrors of war, including the prospect that your life or the life of the person standing next to you could end in the blink of an eye. In a war zone, that's the life a soldier leads, everyday. Humor can help a soldier maintain his or her sanity.

My name is Jim McCue and I'm a comedian from Boston. Since 1999, my friend Joey Carroll (another Boston comedian) and I have had the privilege of traveling to overseas military bases, and have been given the mission of providing a respite to the men and women who bravely risk their lives in service to their country.

This is a collection of observations from annual or twice-a-year tours to war zones in Bosnia, Kosovo, Afghanistan, and Iraq. From my first booking, the experience has had a profound effect on me.

In comedy, like a lot of jobs, we use jargon to describe events. If a show goes well, we say the comedian "killed." If it doesn't, he "bombed" or "died."

I used to use those terms without thinking. I don't anymore.

Chapter One

Joey Carroll & Jim McCue

    I'm not crazy about flying, so I ask God for some courage and climb aboard. The flight is extremely crowded. The crew chief has to have people make room to fit everyone in. The C 130 is a prop plane, not built for comfort. Passengers sit on benches with cargo and with netting as back support. The back half of this very open area is filled with pallets piled with luggage and other cargo. It feels and sounds like we are traveling in a cement mixer. We all wear earplugs and communication outside of hand signals is futile. After a two-and-a-half-hour flight, the C 130 does what is called a combat landing, dropping and swerving so as to not give potential bad guys an easy or predictable flight path to target. I get nervous, but being surrounded by soldiers who seem bored makes me feel better. I certainly don't want to look like a wimp, so I try to keep my poker face as we touch down.

    A ramp at the rear of the plane lowers hydraulically. First

the pallets are offloaded with a forklift. Then we passengers walk down the ramp. Hello Iraq. It is dusk at Camp Diamondback.

I am carrying a duffle bag and backpack and my first steps on Iraqi soil are rather clumsy ones. We head off to the left where various Point of Contact (POC) personnel are looking for their passengers. About thirty soldiers are separated from our herd and immediately processed. Someone from Morale, Welfare & Recreation (MWR) sticks a hand out and asks if I am one of the comedians. I guess word went down range that I'm six-foot-six. The fact that I'm dressed as a civilian also helps me stand out in the crowd. I am wearing a t-shirt and Kevlar body armor with a helmet. The Kevlar does not fit very well. I guess they don't have a Big-and-Tall Kevlar Store in this country.

Joey Carroll's Kevlar has an additional flap to protect his crotch, which is aptly named a "ball flap". I guess the army does not value my balls as highly as I do.

Joey, Jeff Davidson, the Lieutenant, and I shake hands with three or four people who are all very gracious. From research online, I know that Camp Diamondback is a 500-soldier base camp similar to what U.S. forces occupy in the Balkans, located at Mosul Airport.

We check in, and meet an officer who also happens to be the "mayor" of Diamondback. He is a strapping guy with a firm handshake. I must confess I'm not sure how soldiers become mayors of these bases, but know they are people who get things done. He tells us that this is a good time in that they haven't had a rocket or mortar attack in four days. I worry that might mean we are due for one, but find out later that the insurgents don't like to attack in bad weather.

By the rivers of mud outside that used to be road, it's obvious that the weather has been crappy. We drop our gear in the sleeping quarters and head to the dining facility. It is very dark. The whole camp keeps the lights of cars and houses blacked out so the insurgents do not get a good target. It reminds me of stories I have heard about World War II when people would keep their lights low and paint the top half of their headlights so the enemy would not be able to target towns and cities in the U.S.

I'm grateful for a flashlight I picked up somewhere in my travels. I cup the end of the flashlight with my hand so only enough light is used so I can see the path in front of me. When we finally get to the dining facility, the food is great.

Someone notices my camera bag and asks me how I got it into the dining facility. I just carried it in.

"Really," says the soldier, "I'm surprised. This is where the bomb killed all of those soldiers."

The pictures of all those dead and wounded soldiers flash through my mind. I don't know if you remember this, but a terrorist brought a bomb into this dining facility and set it off, killing himself and a bunch of others. I'm a little distracted and lose my appetite. But as I look around, everyone continues to talk about the weather, the mud, our flight, and a celebrity court case that's been in the news back home. We finish our meals and go straight to the theater. It's almost show time.

But I'm getting ahead of myself. Let's start at the beginning. I was in Los Angeles, at a comedy club…

Chapter Two

What do you wear to a war?

Soldiers might have their own ideas when they pack their belongings for a one-year deployment, but this is what a comedian brings for a 30-day military tour:

4 Sweatshirts
4 Sweaters
10 T-shirts
10 Pairs of underwear
5 Pairs of pants
1 Pair of sneakers
1 Pair of flip-flops for showers
1 Pair of hiking boots
1 Passport
1 Digital camera
1 Video camera
1 Mini disc recorder
3 Chargers
Film
Shaving kit
Vitamins
Zinc …

That's it, plus my itinerary, all stuffed into a rolled-up duffel bag and a backpack that bulges so that it looks like I stuffed Santa Claus into a tube sock. It seems particularly bulky when you're bouncing over rough terrain in a Hummer or when your Black Hawk helicopter is making sharp turns at 100 feet of altitude.

I am with Joey Carroll, another Boston comedian and my regular traveling partner. Because of security issues, we're not exactly sure where we're going. We know that it's somewhere in Iraq and Kuwait, and beyond that we have to trust in the U.S. military. I am comfortable with that.

What I'm not comfortable about is that I have a head cold, and know from experience how exhausting these tours can be. This is my sixth one, and I usually end up sick by the end. Some of the comedians who've done this gig have told me that you have to be a little sick to take this gig in the first place. For the next thirty days, Joey and I will be jostled around in all types of transportation, at all hours, sometimes sharing a bench seat with a fellow holding an M-16. We'll be catnapping in makeshift quarters, told when to wake up, when to eat, where to go and what to do. And there's a pretty good chance somebody's going to lob a bomb or shoot at us. It's happened before.

All of which, I know, is nothing compared to what the soldiers are going through. Our little vacation serves as a reminder not just of their sacrifice, but as a reminder that they make that sacrifice so that I can live the life I do -- sleeping late and eating cereal in front of a television set.

Right now, I'm feeling anxious because I will be out of contact with my civilian world. I can only imagine the stress on the military personnel beginning an entire tour of duty, which is a year in duration. But that's something to focus on for another time, because right now I'm focused on getting an exit row on the airplane. I'm 6-foot-6, so getting the exit row is important if I want leg room for a long flight. The exit row is the poor man's first class. If I sit in the middle seat, I feel like a giraffe stuffed into a coffee can.

So far, war is hell.

Chapter Three

The trip from Joey Carroll's house near Boston's Logan Airport to Frankfurt, Germany, is seventeen hours. We stroll around the airport in Germany for most of our three-hour layover, trying to keep from falling asleep and missing our connection to Vienna. By the time we fall asleep, it will be 5:30 a.m., assuring that our body clocks will be completely altered.

At the Vienna Airport, we hook up with Jeff Davidson, the stage manager assigned to us by AKA Productions, which booked the tour. We jump onto another plane, this time bound for Kosovo. I've spoken with Jeff on the phone and he seems like a good guy. I guess he used to manage the band War. I'm sure he will have great stories to tell. War stories; Get it?

Great; only twenty four hours into this trip and I'm telling puns. Please don't burn this book.

Kosovo is cold this time of year. When we get through customs, our armed escort is waiting for us. It's an odd feeling, to have an armed escort. It could easily lead one to develop a false sense of importance. On the other hand, it could also identify one as a target worth shooting at.

On one of my previous trips, I flew into Sarajevo and the schedules were messed up. I had to walk about a quarter of a mile and inform a very surprised American soldier that I needed him to call the NATO base and let them know the comedian was here and needed a ride.

Like I said, some things can lead one to develop a false sense of importance.

As we approach the gates of Fort Bondsteel in Kosovo, I take out my military papers and identification. You need both to be allowed on base and to be issued a more official military ID. As I pull out my papers, I find a check I thought I had deposited before leaving. This is bad, because I have written checks out to pay bills that will bounce. On the base, Jeff hooks us up via internet and I am able to have another check issued.

My girlfriend will have to deposit the check as soon as possible.

It is February 14. "Happy Valentine's Day," I think.

While frustrating, the experience gives me an appreciation of how difficult it must be for our troops to manage their finances while stationed abroad, particularly those who have left better paying jobs to serve their country.
I know two absolute truths about this war.

First, the bills don't stop because you are deployed. Second, if Osama Bin Laden owed money to American Express, we would know where that bastard was hiding.

Chapter Four

When we arrive at the airport, Joey and I stick out like sore thumbs. We are picked up by a soldier from Southern Ohio, who gives us an armed escort from Camp Bondsteel to Camp Montieth, where we will perform tonight. We are surprised to find out that Joey and the soldier know the same guy from his small home town in Southern Ohio. When I say small, I mean 200 people -- total population -- small. The soldier can't wait to e-mail his wife to tell her about their mutual friend and what a small world it is.

Aside from getting soldiers to laugh at our shows, these encounters with individual serviceman are a big part of our job. I have worked clubs all over the U.S. and can often share a common memory of a city or town near home for these soldiers. In some small way, knowing where the best cheese steak or pizza place is brings these men and women a little closer to home, even if it's just for a moment.

Soldiers also have become a great source of material. I met a soldier once and he would say everything is "Outstanding!"

How are you doing? "Outstanding!"

How's the food? "Outstanding!"

How are the sleeping quarters? "Outstanding!"

He became part of my act.

"I just took a two-pound crap."

"Outstanding!"

Chapter Five

Jim McCue, Camp Monteith

We start out for Camp Montieth, which, according to Globalsecurity.org, incorporates a former Serb Army post with more than two miles of perimeter fence, housing one armored battalion and one infantry battalion. The base camp was established in June 1999 in Kosovo to be used as staging points for the bulk of U.S. forces stationed in the Multi National Brigade-East.

I am really happy to see the Camp's Morale, Welfare & Recreation resident manager, Tony. Over the years, we have developed a friendship.

Tony tells us he's divorcing his third wife and marrying wife number four. It must be hard to maintain relationships at this distance, I think, but I'm still not going to get him a wedding gift. Three marriages is my limit, I tell him.

For the trip to the base, the Morale, Welfare & Recreation staff, Jeff, Joey, and I will ride in a white van. Traveling in front and behind us are Hummers with four soldiers in each vehicle. When I first came through Kosovo in 2000, a machine gunner would man the small turret located on the top of the Hummer. The first time I rode this way, I thought that if I was the enemy, which target would I aim for?

Obviously, I would shoot at the comedians in the white van.

Luckily for these soldiers, now that the violence has calmed down they do not have to man the turrets on this cold, wet, raw day. Driving around with half your body sticking out of the roof of a moving vehicle must be painful in the winter. Even in good weather, it would suck getting hit in the mouth with a June bug.

Chapter Six

After the show, we drive home in our convoy and discuss the most annoying sitcom theme song. Joey notes the number of lights we can see in the Kosovo night skyline, a sign that things are improving here. When we first came through the Balkans in 1999, many of the buildings were burnt out or reduced to rubble, and at night there was little light on the horizon. It's a good thing to see this part of the world healing as a direct result of something our country has done.

Later, I realize that it's not so great to try to sleep with the song from the Brady Bunch playing over and over in your head.

Chapter Seven

Jim McCue & Joey Carroll prove comedians watch too many cartoons

The MWR has Thai massage available at the gym. Joe and I get one-hour Thai massages for only twenty dollars. I am hoping the masseuse will untie some of the knots I acquired while flying in steerage. The Thai woman weighs about sixty pounds and she bends my 6-foot-6 frame like a pretzel. I'm not sure if she was trying to relax me or obtain military secrets, but I gave her the secret hiding place of my sling shot and my social security number.

At 8 p.m., it's show time. The show takes place in a large metal building that serves as the base gymnasium. One half is filled with weights and the other half is a basketball court with a stage along one sideline.

The hall is packed with about 300 soldiers. Joey opens and "kills" for about forty five minutes. I close out the show. It's a great crowd.

You can't see anyone lifting weights, but every so often you can hear the grunt from a soldier pushing out one more rep. I try to time my jokes so the sound of "arraahhh" coming from the weight room is muffled by laughter. I started my career in clubs that closely resemble men's rooms, so this is no big problem.

After the show, we sign autographs of our photos, provided by AKA. The soldiers are very appreciative. Then we grab a bite to eat at the mess hall. Life is good.

At 11 p.m. we meet a crew chief from the Cleveland area. Nice guy. He invites us out to his hanger to show off a Black Hawk helicopter and the newest form of night vision goggles.

Someone once told me that one man with an M16 riffle could win the Revolutionary War single handedly. I would rather go back with a slingshot and a pair of night vision goggles. It would take longer, but it would be a lot more fun.

When we get to the hangar, we meet another crew chief who thanks us for our performance. I ask my new friend, who lives outside of Cleveland, what a crew chief does. He explains with a chuckle that he is a "stewardess with a machine gun."

He goes on to explain that he acts as a gunner and is responsible for all of the passengers sitting behind the pilot. He explains with impressive detail the mechanical attributes of the aircraft. I won't remember very much of these details, but I'm comforted by how knowledgeable and well trained these soldiers are. I still can't set the clock on my VCR.

I am also thinking about that image, the "stewardess with a machine gun," which will stick with me whenever I'm on a commercial flight.

Chapter Eight

It's 7:30 a.m. I get up and enjoy breakfast. Several soldiers from last night's show recognize me. I answer several questions about where I am from and how long I have been doing comedy. One soldier comments on how much guts it must take to stand up there on stage. Obviously, he is the braver of the two of us. No matter how tough an audience is, I've never had to bring a rifle to work.

Maybe I should. It would keep the hecklers in line.

Chapter Nine

"Road Rage Rudy"

Two Hummers and eight soldiers escort us to the airport. We say our goodbyes and are off to Bosnia. To get to Bosnia from Kosovo you must fly to Austria first, because a couple of tiny countries with names like "Postagestampistan" do not permit us to use their airspace.

We finally get to Bosnia at 9:30 p.m., which is a little later than we planned, because our plane needed to be de-iced in Vienna. The climate will change dramatically in a few days, when we go to Iraq. We will go from deep snowdrifts to the desert.

After customs, we find two familiar faces waiting to pick us up. Allen "Mac" McNeil, our MWR specialist, and "Road Rage Rudy." Mac likes cold beer and Harley Davidson bikes, and is a decorated tank commander from Desert Storm. He now runs MWR at Camp "Butmir," a NATO Base in Sarajevo. We first met him in 1999 at a base in Tazar, Hungary, the first stop in the Balkans' tour.

He's married a girl who lives in this part of the world and I think they have one child.

Mac has a couple of good stories and some advice about what not to step on; landmines, mostly. Every year, he reminds me that there are almost one million unexploded mines in Bosnia. "Please stay on the hard top," he says.

"Road Rage Rudy" is a German tour bus driver who is a legend to almost every entertainer who has performed for our troops. He is an amiable guy, but in a traffic jam you are likely to hear some colorful phrases not taught in German Language Class 101.

As we drive down the two-lane road in Bosnia, where horse carts are still a common mode of transportation, we can hear genuine German dialect, and Rudy.

Lesson one is "Shizen," which he will tell you in German means "good driver."

Chapter Ten

UXO stands for unexploded ordinance

At 6:30 a.m., at the base in Bosnia, I wake up with a headache. The heat in my sleeping quarters is very dry and it is about eighty degrees. I think that does a number on my sinuses.

My head pounds, and I imagine the conversation.

"Did anything bad happen while you were in Bosnia?"

"Yes," I reply. "My sinuses were killing me."

Plus I forgot my favorite pillow and Teddy Bear.

I decide to keep my sinuses to myself, and thank God for another day of life.

My thoughts go to my cousin Rick and his son Casey. I'm trying to meet up with Casey in Iraq. Casey is stationed in Camp War Eagle in Sadr City, Baghdad and is with the first Calvary, CFSC 115th unit 9008.

My clearest memories of Casey were from when he was a boy, a good kid. I asked one of the folks at AKA Productions to find out if it is possible to get us together for a show or possibly a cup of coffee. I also gave this information to my tour manager who will ask our POC person if there is a way to make it happen.

The look on Jeff's face when he reads the address tells me my chances aren't good.

"Sadr City, that's a hot spot," he says. "We can give it a try, but that's rough, man."

Casey has been there for more than a year and is due to return home sometime within the next month. I have not seen Casey in about 10 years. I'm not sure what we will talk about. "So, remember when you were learning to ride your bike without training wheels?"

I guess I'll play it by ear.

At 8 a.m. I wake Joey. We grab some breakfast, pack for one night, and it's off to Eagle Base, a two-and-a-half-hour drive through very mountainous terrain. This will be the first time for me that Rudy's tour bus is not protected by armed escorts, which is another sign that things have improved here since the NATO military intervention in 1995. It has taken several years for the country to reach this point of stability. I hope the violence in Iraq does not take that long to end, but have a feeling that it will.

As we drive out of Sarajevo, you can still see that many of the houses and buildings are destroyed. Many have been reduced to rubble. Some still have bullet holes in the walls. But because we have passed this way in other years, we can see that a lot of the bullet holes have been mended. There are some new buildings now.

One of those structures that has been rebuilt is the building that houses the region's newspaper. It always stuck in my mind, after being shelled heavily during the siege of Sarajevo. I always thought that it looked like a giant -- possibly one with a grudge against its editorial practices -- had smashed the top floors with a giant fist.

As we drive past, I entertain the hope that all the hatred between the different factions of people will mend as well. The cynic in me doubts it. These people have a hatred that goes back hundreds of years. Why can't humans be unified and pick the same things to hate, I think, like telemarketers.

We meet with Colonel Peterson at 9 a.m. He has been called out of retirement to serve at this NATO base. He thanks us for coming and as we chitchat, he tells us that a mine just outside the base's perimeter killed a dog. This is a reminder that there are still over a million unexploded mines in Bosnia. Mac's warning sounds in my head: "Stay on the hardtop."

With size fourteen shoes, I'm a natural minesweeper.

Chapter Eleven

AKA Tour manager Jeff Davis, Joey Carroll & Jim McCue

The trip from Sarajevo is over a long, windy, mountainous road. This country looks quite beautiful with all of the fresh snow covering the trees. Many of the burned-out houses and cars look less foreboding now that over a foot of fresh snow covers them like frosting. I could go for a slice of my girlfriend Bernadette's chocolate cake right now.

This beautiful country was host to the Winter Olympics in 1984. I was told that snipers used the luge runs to kill civilians. I guess that is about the darkest irony I can imagine, a shift from the Olympic spirit to the killing of civilians while they try to fetch water or bury the dead.

With about one hour yet to go to reach our destination we stop at a small restaurant. I've been here before. It's a regular stop for Rudy and the people working here welcome us warmly. We order Bosnian coffee, which has a potency that makes cappuccino seem like cocoa. It comes in a double shot-glass-sized cup. We all get a big laugh when Joey downs the whole thing like a shot. The coffee leaves about a half an inch of mud in the bottom, which even the heartiest of coffee addicts will not touch.

The look on Joey's face as this low thirty weight coffee sludge rolls over his tongue is priceless. He looks like he is trying to swallow a live mouse. Of course, Joey is willing to do what it takes for the laugh, so he downs my coffee sludge as well.

As we exit the restaurant, I notice about five puppies, only two of which are brave enough to come over to play. They very nervously accept our affection, obviously hoping for a handout. Rudy starts yelling, "Back on!" for everyone to get back on the bus. I think his Bosnian coffee is kicking in. Before we leave, we venture into the men's room. This room doesn't have toilets, only holes in the floor. The stench is so bad that I get a laugh when I say, I never thought I would miss the smell of ass.

Chapter Twelve

Cold welcome for Joey Carroll & Jim McCue

Eagle base has changed a lot since I first came here in 1999. It is now populated by a mix of American and European soldiers. Our credentials are waiting for us at the gate. We head in and drive to the dining facility, or 'difac' (pronounced dee fac). It seems ironic that there is both a European and American dining facility, and virtually everyone eats at the American one. This is either a tribute to the culinary skills of the U.S. military, or an indication that no one is sending the best French chefs to the Bosnia.

In the interests of diplomacy and because we may come this way again, we call it a tribute to U.S. military cooks.

After we eat, we go to the PX and check our emails. We are welcomed to the base by a civilian contractor in charge of the bases. He explains that many civilians hired by the Department of Defense are now doing jobs once performed by a soldier. He has only been on this base for two weeks, which means that if you count the seven trips I've made to this base, I have actually been here longer than he has. (Note to self: I need to spend more time in NY and LA. I think the chances of me getting discovered in Bosnia are slim).

My first trip to the Eagle was a much different experience, in 1999. We did twenty to twenty five shows in the Balkans. Now we're doing only two because there are fewer soldiers. I recall there being more than 10,000 American troops, maybe 3,000 about a mile away at a base called Comanche. I met my first four-star general that year. I was waiting in a shower line wearing sweatpants and a tee-shirt carrying a shaving kit and towel under my arm. I was obviously the only American civilian. A sergeant walked up to me and asked me rather officially if I was James W. McCue. This was the first person outside of my mother who used my entire name and she only did that when I did something to try her patience.

"Yes, I am."

He told me to come with him, and that General Clark would like to see me.

"Did someone in my family die?"

"No, General Clark just wants to welcome you to the base."

"Great," I said, relieved. "I'll take a shower and change into something more presentable to meet a general."

"No," the sergeant corrected. I was to go directly with him.

The other comic with me on that trip was John McDonnell. We found him, also wearing sweat pants, and headed to the "White House."

The "White House" is a building within an eagle base ringed in barbed wire and security. It houses the offices of the top brass. We arrived and security proceeded to search us, picking through my shaving kit, before directing us to a waiting room. (As they picked through the contents of my shaving kit, I tried to determine whether there'd be anything embarrassing they might pull out. I was relieved and a little surprised when there wasn't).

After about thirty minutes, Gen. Wesley Clark bustled out and welcomed us to his office. He was in great spirits, and cheerfully told us that laughter is good for the morale.

He pulled out a map of the theater -- not the one where we'd do the show, but the one where they were waging a war. He gave us a quick explanation of his military strategy, and asked for our opinion.

Just kidding.

What he did do was deliver a concise but informative talk about the history of the areas, running back to the Middle Ages and finishing with modern-day ethnic cleansing. As he talked, I couldn't pull my attention away from the four stars on the guy's collar. Growing up the son of a marine, I'd always thought of a four-star general as being akin to the Loch Ness Monster or Bigfoot. You heard of their existence, but no one ever really saw one. I thought they stayed at the Pentagon or N.O.R.A.D or something. Gen. Clark finished up a very knowledgeable and informative talk about the history of the area from the Middle Ages to modern-day ethnic cleansing.

When the general finished, he asked if we had any questions. I took the opportunity to apologize for our appearance, showing him my shaving kit and towel as proof that we would have liked to be more presentable. He laughed and explained that when he sends for someone, that person is delivered as promptly as possible. Apparently, the sergeant was not about to tell a four-star general that the comedian would get to him when he got around to it.

Chapter 13

Jim McCue & Allen McNeil "Mac" poses with me in Sarajevo.

We check out our performance space, a 50-seat MWR facility. It's much smaller than "Trigger," a room from my first trip that fit 600 soldiers. The space looks fine though. Mike, the MWR guy who runs the facility, promises to scrounge up a few microphones for the sound systems. We agree to be back at 7:30 for an eight o'clock show.

I go back to the "Audie Murphy," the temporary billeting facility where we will be staying tonight, three to a room. I lay on a bed and drop right to sleep. I'm really suffering from a cold. It's in my lungs and head and gives me that groggy, weightless feeling you get when your sinuses are stuffed with concrete. Audie Murphy was the highest decorated soldier in the history of the Army who went on to become a movie star. I doubt he would let a stuffy nose keep him from performing, even if he was an actor. I'm awakened by Jeff at 7 p.m. He's afraid to let me sleep any longer for fear we'd be late for the show. I quickly wash my face, brush my teeth, and jump in the van to do the show.

At 7:30, I order the last thing left on the menu, "Trigger's Triple Deluxe." If you ever find yourself at eagle base, I highly recommend it. The soldiers come trickling in and we end up with around thirty soldiers in attendance, all but one of them a civilian. The show goes great and almost all of them ask for and receive autographed pictures. I'm amazed at how much fun you can have with just thirty people at a show.

Then we go to the defac. All I can eat is turkey noodle soup. The broth tastes like it might have healing qualities. I hope I don't get Jeff and Joey sick.

Audie Murphy might think I'm a sissy, but he would appreciate my thoughtfulness.

Chapter Fourteen

*Jim McCue poses in hand dug tunnel used to
keep Sarajevo alive during siege.*

We wake up, eat and hit the road back from to Tuzla Sarajevo. The road is beautiful; and there is a windy, snow-covered mountainous landscape that cannot be captured by our cameras or my limited ability to describe it. Along the way we pass destroyed, burnt-out houses, but between the snow and the other forces of nature that have worked on the area over the past several years, the casual observer might assume these dwellings were abandoned. We have U2 playing on the bus, and as we drive through the picturesque but war-torn countryside we listen to "It's a Beautiful Day."

It's surreal, but it fits.

Rudy is bringing us back to Camp Butmir and making good time. We convince Mac to let Rudy bring us to "The Tunnel." During the siege of Sarajevo, the Bosnians used only hand tools like picks and shovels to create an 800-meter tunnel under the airport, which was used to bring food and medicine to a starving city. It was also used to bring out the wounded. The Serbs knew of its location and periodically poured mortars and sniper bullets into the area, taking many lives, but were never able to permanently shut it down. It is a powerful place.

Back on the base, we go to a place called Sammy's to perform for troops at Butmir. Sammy's is more of a dive saloon than a comedy club. The soldiers on this base are allowed to drink alcohol and those who attended the show at Sammy's took full advantage, making the performance a difficult one. The majority of the allied forces in the audience are from England, Germany, Italy and France. They do not expect a comedy show when they walk through the door, just a normal night of drinking in the pub.

At home, we would call this a "Hell gig." The longer you're in comedy, the better you become, the more you try to avoid venues like this.

Joey is unflappable. The room is loud with chatter, but he delivers like a pro. There is a heavyset female contractor who is blatantly competing with Joey for the attention of the soldiers. She continues to go from male to male, tapping them on the shoulder while trying to strike up conversation. Joey ignores her and gets pretty respectable laughs giving the cards he is dealt.

Then it is my turn. Just as I am introduced, about nineteen British soldiers walk in. They are drunk. I make a generic statement about how with a male-female ration of 1,000-to-1, a 200-pound female starts to look like a super model. It gets a big laugh, and the obnoxious big lady takes the hint and quiets down. I am settling into my act when I get heckled from one of my British friends. I ask the crowd to give our English friends a round of applause, then I compliment them on being one of our only allies. Then I told them I have met the queen…. nice guy. This also gets a big laugh.

I wish I could say that the line turns the room around -- that the crowd quiets down and listens and we all enjoy an evening of laughter -- but it doesn't go that way. I do the rest of my act and survive it, but no one seems to care about the show.

It's a funny thing about gigs like this, though. While Joey and I know it is nothing like the rest of our shows, six soldiers approach us after the show and ask for autographs. They tell us that we made their night.

I know it sounds trite, but that makes it worthwhile.

Chapter Fifteen

There is a sign at the NATO base in Sarajevo stating clearly that there is alcohol being served, so don't bring your gun after six.

My joke: They say guns don't kill people, people kill people. Guns make it a hell of a lot easier though. When is the last time you heard of a drive-by stoning?

Of course now they want to pass a law that forces people to put child locks on their guns. You know what this means? Only children will be able to operate firearms.

Parent: "Bed time."

Click.

Child: "I don't think so…"

Chapter Sixteen

Joey Carroll travel face.

We have a couple of travel days. On the first, we travel eight hours from Bosnia to Vienna to Heathrow, England. We get to see the airport and hotel. On the second, we travel sixteen hours, from England to Kyrgyztan. We are amazed at the time it takes. I have a middle seat. Not to belabor this, but I'm six-foot-six, so sitting in a middle seat for that long is like being locked in the stocks in medieval times.

On the bright side, when I finally get the chance to stand up, it feels wonderful. And the hotel back in England serves a great breakfast.

Chapter Seventeen

Jim McCue home away from home in Kyrgyzstan.

After sixteen hours folded into my airplane seat, we arrive at the Manas International Air Base in Kyrgyzstan. I wake up after just five hours, so decide that it's laundry time. When doing these tours, whenever you have the opportunity to eat, sleep or do your laundry, you take it. Clean underwear is next to Godliness.

We were supposed to get today off, but Sergeant Dan Sharp tells us the venue we will be performing in will be used to bunk incoming troops, so asks if we can move our show up a night. We're up for that; it's not like we have anything else to do. He also asks if we can add a midnight show for the military police that are on patrol and will miss the first show. We're glad to do it. That's what we are here for.

(Joke: If you ever get pulled over by a cop and he asks you to walk that straight line don't stop to take a piss. They hate that.)

The first show goes great with maybe 500 or 600 soldiers

in attendance. Before we go up, the sergeant reminds us that we should not do anything offensive during our performance. The week before, a comedian who shall remain nameless managed to offend a few of the officers and the chaplain (although he still had a great set). Sergeant Sharp was pleasant and even a little apologetic, but made sure we knew they did not find any of the seven dirty words or ethnic or sexually explicit material acceptable.

I work clean so this was one of those times that I was thankful that I did not work blue. Of course, this still provides Joey and me with the opportunity to torture the sergeant by asking if this swear or that swear is OK, with each one fouler then the one before. At first he looks a little panicked, but as we build on the vulgarity of each curse, he catches on to the gag and laughs good naturedly.

The hip hop/gospel group Set Free performs after us. Joey and I take this opportunity to get some coffee and check our emails. At the base coffee shop, we discover that we can call the States for nineteen cents a minute. I make some calls as Joey Carroll hangs out with a group of soldiers who had been at the show. When I came back, it frees up a phone for Joey, and it is my turn to hold court with the soldiers.

I enjoy meeting these men and women who serve our country and protect our freedoms. They really are the very best our nation has to offer. They ask about their favorite comedians. Although I cannot say I'm friends with all of the top comedians, in many cases I have opened for or had some friendly encounter with them.

A lot of comedians can remember a ton of street jokes, but I cannot. When people find out you are a comedian they of course want to hear something funny. As I frequently do, I find myself remembering that I need to learn a few street jokes for situations like this. Sometimes soldiers tell me jokes or about funny situations they think will work well with my act. But nothing gives them more joy then watching me make good-natured fun of their fellow soldiers from the stage. I just ask them what they do for the military and I can usually do something based on their job.

When Joey comes back from the phones, it is obvious to me that he received some bad news from the states. He found out his sister, who had been ill, passed away two days prior to Joey's phone call. When Joey committed to this trip he knew his sister was in failing health. He visited her in the hospital to say good-bye, but there is really no way to prepare for news like this.

On top of this, I know that today is Joey's birthday.

Just a few minutes earlier, I mentioned that news to Sergeant Sharp, who grabbed the news with great zeal and left in search of a birthday cake.

Joey returns to the table, and it is obvious to me that he's distracted. He's a good guy, and was close to his sister, and he's grieving.

And seemingly out of nowhere, in walks Sergeant Sharp with eight or so soldiers, a piece of cake, and a ridiculously oversized birthday candle. They are all singing "Happy Birthday."

Joey is just shocked. For one thing, I think that he forgot it was his birthday and secondly he is surprised that anyone re-membered. With all of us sitting around joining in singing happy birthday to him, Joey responds with a big smile. He is stunned, and once more I think that while we make these trips to boost the mo-rale of the soldiers, it is frequently the soldiers who make us feel warmth, happiness, and pride.

Later, I tell Joey that I can cover his time for the late show if he wants to sit one out.

"No," he tells me. "This is what I'm here for."

We go back to the tent, for our unscheduled late show for a group of overtired military police. As I introduce Joey, it occurs to me that even a comedian can be a hero. Joey swallows the loss of his sister and has a great set. For those thirty minutes, he relieves the stress and boredom of these soldiers by replacing it with laughter.

Chapter Eighteen

Jim McCue & Joey Carroll meet the good folks guarding the base.

I wake up and walk through the early-morning snow in my leather coat and flip-flops. En route to the latrine, I wipe the sleep from my eyes and notice that a wild dog is standing in my path.

It is a dark dog, smaller than a German shepherd, long haired and alert. It pants heavily, hungrily, as it contemplates me.

"Great," I think. "This is just what I need, to fight off this dog with my size fourteen flip flops."

In my black leather coat and shorts, I look like a biker version of Big Bird.

I do my best to stare down the dog, but when he turns and runs off I think he might have just decided that my pale, skinny legs don't look appetizing no matter how long it's been since his last meal. My legs have had the same effect on women.

Joey and I take a tour of the base, and meet many of the soldiers who had been to the show the night before. We start with the military police, stationed at the gates and at small, fortified posts. Joey is wearing a gaudy gold running suit and there is an African American female who gets a huge bang out of his outfit. She can't stop giggling. In his act, Joey has a line: "I know what you're thinking... somewhere there is a pimp freezing his ass off."

The MPs who man the gates for twelve hour shifts have it pretty tough. Their exposure to the weather alone would make that job a grind. They are very gracious and happy to meet us, and tell us which lines made them laugh at last night's show.

Next, we take a tour of the fire station. They give us a ride on their fire truck and show us their jaws of life, and seem just like the firemen we meet back home, although they're wearing camouflage. These guys inspire some new material, about how I would never have the guts to be a fireman. I would show up and say, "Sorry, you are going lose the house ...

"I'm not going in there...

"I'll buy you a new cat ....

"Let's face it -- your grandmother was getting kind of old."

At our next stop, we meet Col. Glass, the number two man on the base. He tells us that sometimes as many as 30,000 people pass through that base on their way to one place or another. That is pretty impressive, considering they all need to be fed and housed. We sign a flag that all the entertainers are asked to sign, and I can't help but wonder if there will some day be some big celebrity signing that flag and saying, "Who the hell is Jim McCue?"

Col. Glass tells me that his goal is to leave the base better then he found it for the next group of troops stationed here, a great philosophy. That's something all of us might want to think about the next time we drop a piece of litter on a park lawn, or blast our crappy music from car radios as we sit in traffic.

At our next stop we meet engineers, purchasing agents, and accountants; all important members of this team that makes the base run efficiently. Throughout the day, we meet people and wait for information about when we fly to Afghanistan.

At 4:30 p.m. we still do not have any information about when or even where our next show will take place. Just before 5 p.m., we hear we might have to ship out at 6. This is a little stressful because we need to get back to our tent and pack. Then we are told that the flight will leave at 3 a.m. Then we find out that we fly out at 6 p.m. tomorrow. With that news in our heads, we go to sleep, feeling like Bill Murray in Goundhog Day.

Chapter Nineteen

Every comedian should have their own bomb squad.

It is Goundhog Day. That is, it is morning and I am walking through the snow in flip-flops, headed to the latrines and a morning shower. I wonder what happened to that dog.

My cold seems to be getting better, thanks to some multivitamins and a good night's sleep. My girlfriend Bernadette packed the multivitamins, so I make a mental note to appreciate her more and stop at the PX to buy her a card. I also buy myself some sunglasses.

Today, Joey and I get to meet the bomb squad. I'm sure the Air Force has a slightly different name for this group, but these people are responsible for finding and disposing of unexploded ordnance. Bombs.

Because I am always interested in matching personality types to different professions, I can't help wondering what these soldiers were like as little kids, particularly around the 4th of July.

They let me try on a bomb suit, and I waddle around in it like a half-assed astronaut. The suite is heavy, but not as heavy as I expected. The soldier explains that old suits were about ninety pounds and this one is only sixty. Next they show us a "water cannon," which is not your typical super soaker but is very cool. It uses a 50-caliber shell to create a concentrated beam of water that can disable or detonate a bomb from a safe distance.

It would be a great thing to have around the house, in case you ever needed to settle a disagreement with your neighbor.

The bomb unit also breaks out its version of R2D2. It is a robotic bomb technician which makes it safer for these soldiers to do their job. Simply put, if they can send a robot, controlled at a safe distance by a human, they won't need to send humans.

I wish I'd had a robot like this for my prom, I think. Probably, so would have my prom date.

Chapter Twenty

No trip is complete without a picture in a stupid hat.

We are awakened at 07:30 -- 7:30 a.m. to you civilians --- and told that we have one hour to shower, eat, and pack before we hop a plane to Afghanistan. We hustle to do so, and then for the next eight hours we wait to see if we have been cleared to go.

At about 16:30 -- 4:30 p.m. to you civilians -- we learn we will not be flying out today. Again today, it's Groundhog Day.

There are many new faces on base. The Korean Army is being replaced and we have a lot of US Army personnel passing through the base on their way to Afghanistan. Every bunk on base is being assigned to someone, and even the tent we performed in is completely filled with cots and soldiers in transit. I'm thankful we still have our bunks. A canvas drop cloth divides the tent into small private rooms. It gives me some privacy, although the flap gives zero protection from snoring. Joey can really saw wood; he sounds like two wart hogs procreating.

I call Bernadette and chitchat for a while. It's nice to hear her voice. I return to find that we have new temporary residents in our tent; three colonels and two Korean officers. I cannot discern the rank of the Korean officers. One of the colonels is a surgeon. I believe he is part of the National Guard. One of the colonels was called out of retirement. He explains that he has a wife twenty years his junior and that they have a four-year-old whom he misses dearly. The third colonel is special operations -- a ranger, I think. He lives in Hawaii. He was in Afghanistan right after 9-11 and I can only imagine the experiences he has endured for our country. This guy is tough.

He tells me about how they do what is called halo drops, where they use individual oxygen masks to parachute down from over 20,000 feet to avoid detection from enemy forces. I tell him that I have been parasailing in the Cayman Islands. I also explain how my training in the martial arts has given me self-defense tools such as the wedgies and the Indian sunburn.

I make a mental note to start working out when I get back to the world.

Chapter Twenty One

Joey Carroll getting big laughs.

I wake up at 9 a.m. and think, "Well, they didn't get us on the 9 a.m. flight." Joey informs me that we will not be flying out today. We eat, I do my laundry, and once again, we stand by for clearance. That's a military way to say that I take a nap.

At 6 p.m. Joey wakes me up. Sergeant Sharp has talked to the colonel. They would like to know if we can do a show after the bingo game is over in the tent used for games. We are happy to do it.

The show is not an easy one. There is a giant television playing in the back of the room. Two pool tables have drawn the attention of a small group of soldiers, and two dart games, and there is a long line of soldiers waiting for the two beers they are allotted on Saturday night. That's a lot of distractions in one room.

When we are on these tours, Joey and I alternate the order of the show, and it is my turn to go first. As a rule of thumb, the first guy always has to work a little harder, because he needs to warm the crowd up, which can sometimes also mean getting their attention.

I do OK, and I do mean just OK. It is not my best, but the people in the front of the tent are laughing. I do twenty minutes and bring out Joey. Joey hammers through another twenty-five minutes and closes his set. We doubt we'll be signing any autographs, but to our amazement, these people are the best. About forty or so form a line for autographs. Each person warmly shakes our hand and graciously thanks us for doing a great show and coming over to entertain them. This is why I do these tours, I think. The people in our armed forces are the best of all.

After the autographs have been signed, I make my way over to the coffee shop on base to see if there is a phone available. I call to wish my mom a happy birthday. She is out celebrating with her sisters, but my dad is home and I can sense concern in his voice. He knows I am going to Iraq. I didn't mention that fact to my mother because I didn't want to worry her. Happy Birthday Mom!

(Joke: My Mom is an Irish cook, which means she can't. "I don't think you boil that turkey, Mom.")

Chapter Twenty Two

Jim McCue finds inspiration in Kyrgyzstan.

Again this morning, I wake up at 9 a.m., and am starting to feel like a comedy refugee. A guy from the bomb squad said that if I come over he will demonstrate the fifty caliber rifle they use to destroy bombs from a distance, so my plan for today is to hit the showers and make my way over to check it out. A side note: I made the base newspaper yesterday. There was a picture and a small mention about last week's show. On my way to the showers I consider the odds of a talent scout from the Tonight Show reading the camp newspaper from Kyrgyzstan.

I run into a soldier who is on his way to church. I didn't even realize today was Sunday, but decide my spiritual self could use a makeover. After showering I head to the chapel, a tent that holds about 120 worshippers. The crowd is standing room only. Today's message is that our problems are often God's way of forging us into being more Christ-like. He gives several examples, including that of a former big league pitcher named Dave Dravecky. Dravecky lost his arm to cancer -- it snapped in two as he was delivering a pitch in a major league game. What seemed like a horrible tragedy changed his life for the better, though. He became a minister and is thankful Christ put him on the path.

His final example comes from his own experience. He was living in San Francisco some years ago and one day was in a hurry to get across the Bay Bridge. Just as he approached the traffic light to cross the bridge, it turned red. Thinking that missing the light had made him late and ruined his day, he was furious. As it turned out, he wasn't getting across that bridge at all that day, because a petroleum truck exploded on the bridge. He realized that if he had made that light, it may have cost him his life.

It made me wonder if there was some higher purpose for getting stranded on this base. Perhaps that purpose was because our planes were used to help soldiers get to where they are needed or get supplies they need. I hoped it wasn't just so some congressman or senator needed our plane to get to a photo shoot.

Chapter Twenty Three

Jim McCue, Sergeant Dan Sharp, & Joey Carroll

There was a soldier in the news. His wife gave birth to quin-tuplets. The Army told the soldier given the circumstances he would not have to go overseas.

Being a brave soldier he said, "Oh no. I want to go overseas."

.

Chapter Twenty Four

Jim McCue

The first question other comedians ask when they find out about my trips to entertain the troops is "How did you get that job?" The answer is that I was hired by a company called AKA Productions out of Los Angeles back in 1999, during the conflict in Bosnia. I had done a set at a club called The Improv in Los Angeles. I'm originally from Boston but I was in L.A. doing what everybody in my business does, trying to put myself in a position so that the right guy (or woman) would see me. The dream we share is that the person who sees you in that club would like my persona enough, or my act, that she (or he) would offer me a sitcom deal, management, a great gig, a showcase in front of industry, a film, or something -- whatever it is that will get me to the next level, and take me down another road. You don't always know what that thing is, and it can also be elusive.

This thing was the adventure of my life.

Joey Carroll, another Boston comedian who would later

become my traveling partner, was also on the show. Joey is a "material" guy, with each set featuring well-crafted words and thoughts delivered as funny, edgy "bits." He's a great comic and one of my best friends. I am more of a "crowd work" comedian. I have plenty of material, but in most sets I like to take a little time out to chat with people in the crowd. I try not to be mean, but to have a little fun when we talk about their jobs, their lives, and anything else that we can have fun with.

Dan Marconi, an AKA booker, approached me after my set.

"Would you like to entertain the troops?"

It wasn't the thing I'd expected, but it was interesting. My dad is a Marine, and I've always been raised with a lot of respect for the military. The money was good -- not great, but comparable to a week's pay in Vegas. He liked that both Joey and I could work without using "blue" language, and thought my interaction with the audience would go over big with the men and women overseas.

"These soldiers are dealing with the pressures of war overseas, not knowing if the guy standing next to them is going to be there the next day, "Dan told me If you get them laughing, it can change their perspective."

From the start, Joey and I both knew that this was not to be just a job, but an adventure.

The following is taken from a letter from AKA Productions telling me what to expect:

"Your job is to lift the spirits and morale of U.S. Armed Forces men and women to help maintain their readiness and effectiveness while serving in defense of our country. All of the troops you entertain are far away from home and their loved ones. They are stationed in a region with the highest threat condition and extreme weather conditions. From the time you leave until your return, you will meet many people, experience demanding travel, jet lag, military regulations, changing weather, different cultures and languages. Preparation and flexibility will be your keys to a successful tour. There are many things you will not have control over, so you must REMAIN FLEXIBLE AND GO WITH THE FLOW!"

That passage -- while explaining exactly what to expect -- comes nowhere near describing the physical push, pull, sleep, wake, drag, stress and adrenalin rush that are all part of an overseas tour of military bases in a war zone. "Some guys can't do it," Dan confided to me. "You need to understand your mission."

On the other hand, he said, some guys return from each trip saying, "It was horrible. When can I go again?"

Here, it might be a good idea to explain what a comedian's life is usually like.

The thing is, the life of most comedians doesn't fit the military model. Tough duty is a bad crowd, and the longest that lasts is the length of your set, which may run anywhere from ten minutes to an hour. We show up at the night club, we make people laugh, and the rest of the day is ours to do what we'd like. A comedian's idea of roughing it is sleeping on a friend's couch, or doing an overnight and sleeping at a flea bed motel. Our idea of an early morning is one that starts before noon.

All of a sudden, that was going to change for Joey and me. We were going to be told where to go, what to do, when to sleep, wake, and eat. From the first trip, we realized how lucky it is that this was the thing that came that night.

Chapter Twenty Five

Today, though, we are doing a lot of waiting as we try to fly out to Germany two days early. Our plan is to go to Iraq and do more shows on that leg of the tour. I wake up at 04:00, which is a time to go to sleep, not wake up. We shower, eat and go to the airport. British airmen who have not received records of our tickets foil our plans. The locals try to scam our tour manager into paying a fee in cash to get us out. It is obviously a shakedown. After a few hours of airport hell we ship back to the base.

Everywhere we go on the base soldiers yell out: "Are you still here?"

"We ought to get you guy's uniforms."

Groundhog Day continues.

I'm learning about another challenge a soldier faces: boredom. It's been one week and I've seen everything about 100 times. After a week here, we do feel like we're becoming friends with some of the soldiers. The bomb squad catches us walking back to our tent and shows us that fifty-caliber sniper rifle used to destroy bombs from a distance. It's pretty impressive. I mail some clothes home, so I won't have to schlep my winter gear through the desert. I get ready for my 4 a.m. wake-up. This time it is really important that we get out. I do not want to have our Iraq schedule get messed up.

I also learn that I may get the opportunity to see my cousin Casey at Fort New York in Kuwait. He is being processed home after his unit has served bravely in one of the most dangerous parts of Baghdad. I would like to see him, but if he can get out, I will thank God he will get home safely.

It is hard for me to believe that Casey is a soldier in harm's way. I still remember him as a little kid. I know my whole extended family is sending Casey and his unit care packages. It will be great when he returns home safely for a home cooked meal.

Chapter Twenty Six

The diesel heater used to warm the tent is broken and it is freezing cold at 4 a.m. Our stuff is packed and we head to the dining facility for breakfast. We track down our road manager who is trying to get the email for our itinerary. The trip to the airport is uneventful, and we pass through customs fairly easily. There is one stop en route to London, where we eat fish and chips in the airport. We marvel a little too much at our good fortune to eat such wonderful British cuisine, and then we're off to Frankfurt to start the final leg of our tour. Unfortunately, after a twenty one-hour travel day, our luggage is missing. I'm now looking at the next fourteen days of travel in Iraq with two pieces of underwear, two pairs of socks, the pants I'm wearing and a sweater.

In the lost baggage department of Frankfurt Airport, a nice enough guy tells me that he doesn't hold out much hope for my bag being recovered. The good news is that they will reimburse me up to fifty percent (or 1,100 euros) for any clothes I need to buy. The bad news is that at 6-foot-6, finding clothes in Europe that I can feel comfortable in proves impossible. Joey and I check the downtown stores for a couple of hours, then grab some lunch and take the train back to the airport. There are no big and tall shops in Germany. Apparently the fatherland does not sell clothes to Bigfoot.

(Joke: People always say, "You're so tall, do you play basketball?" You don't see me going up to fat people saying, "Hey lardass… are you a sumo wrestler?")

We check in with lost baggage. This time a nice lady tells me they are doing everything they can. I ask God to give her a hand. I don't want to get the smelliest guy in Iraq award. (They say there are no atheists in a foxhole. I don't think there are many in lost luggage department either).

Before going to sleep, I watch CNN. An Italian journalist is injured in Iraq. Her car is fired on by U.S. troops, and according to CNN, the Italian President has summoned our ambassador to his offices, saying that someone must be held responsible. This is a very emotional issue because this same journalist was just released after being captured by terrorists. My hunch is that the car she was traveling in did not stop at a checkpoint. With all of the car bombs, our troops are not taking chances with unknown cars. It bothers me that our soldiers are always assumed to be guilty until proven innocent. Obviously our troops have no motive to shoot at our allies. As the story plays out, there is more talk of a speeding car, ignored signals, flashing lights, warning shots, and finally shooting into the engine block. I don't hear anything, but I can't help but wonder why the Italian security force didn't communicate with U.S. troops ahead of time to avoid this incident.

Last time I did one of these tours, while in a coffee shop a German civilian asked me if I was from the United States. I said, "Yes… No one else would have me." He asked me why the prisoners from Afghanistan were not given protection under the Geneva Convention. I thought, "OK, this is great. I need this crap. I'm not exactly setting policy in the States."

He said he would just like to hear an American view point. I said as politely as possible, "In order to be protected by the Geneva Convention you must sign it and agree to follow its rules. The Taliban were skinning people alive and beheading them in a soccer field."

He asked snidely, "Well what about their protection under your constitution?"

"Well, the only people protected by the United States Constitution are United States citizens."

"What about human rights?"

"You're German… you don't get to talk about human rights." That pissed him off.

"You Americans always bring up World War II. How many times are you going to bring that up?"

"Six million more times."

He said something in German and stormed out.

Most of the people in Germany are awesome. I just happened to run into the one German in all of Germany who has a Howard Dean sticker on his Volkswagen.

Chapter Twenty Seven

While we're checking out, Joey spots my bag. God has answered my prayer. Lufthansa has found my bag! Next stop: Kuwait.

About seven hours later, we arrive in Kuwait at the same time as a half-dozen or so very attractive singers and dancers, former professional sports cheerleaders. They make quite an impression walking through the airport, where almost everyone is an Arabic male. Some are dressed in suits, some in traditional Kuwaiti garb, and all seem fixated on these very, very American women. As we follow them, I say to Joey, "You know, everyone here thinks we're carrying their luggage."

(Cheerleaders have super powers over soldiers that you have to see to believe. I have witnessed a soldier dive over military police to get on stage for a moment with the cheerleaders).

We are met in the airport by about six people, soldiers and some MWR representatives. While they are all in civilian clothes, I notice that many of our escorts are armed. I'm getting used to armed escorts but these guys are in civilian clothes and have side arms. I get the feeling that they do not want to draw too much attention to the Americans leaving the airport. This is an exercise in futility. It would be easier to bring an elephant out of the airport then to get the cheerleaders out without drawing attention.

The luggage is thrown into the back of a pick-up truck. Our group piles into three huge Suburban SUV's that look like something in which ambassadors or heads of state are transported. We get to the base in about twenty minutes. The highway is beautiful; all the signs are in English and Arabic. You cannot tell that there was a war fought here. I guess the Kuwaiti people had the wealth to make repairs, as opposed to the Bosnian people who don't have the oil money.

This base looks more like an industrial park. I'm told it was once just a shipyard. At the final check point on base, we are all asked to get out of the Suburban while they check out the vehicles using mirrors and dogs. A line of buses bringing troops who have been deployed for about a year drives by. You can see all of their faces pushed up against the windows as they see a group of attractive women standing by the side of the road. The soldiers start waving and even though the windows are closed, I am quite sure there is a lot of yelling and whistling. One of the ladies responds by jumping up and down and waving back, which creates even more activity in the bus. We all laugh.

We check into our quarters. The men are in one area and the females in another. The ladies decide to eat at the base burger joint. They are doing four shows tomorrow before going to Iraq. The guys who are with us decide to wait until the midnight meal at the dining facility. It is probably sixty degrees as we walk to the dining facility. I appreciate this weather after the nine days spent schlepping around in the snow and mud in Kyrgyzstan.

When we arrive at the dining facility I am surprised to see about 1,000 soldiers waiting in line to eat at midnight. Once the facility opens, remarkably, it only takes about twenty-five minutes to get inside and eat. The food is great, and I eat a little too much. As I look around at all the faces I realize I cannot even imagine what their life has been like for the past year. Most have been deployed in Iraq. The mood is great, though. Almost any attempt at small talk leads to the soldier saying with a smile, "I'm going home."

I'm happy for them.

We return to our sleeping quarters made up of three modest rooms all connected together. We have our own bathroom, and a washer and a dryer. The quarters are furnished with six bunk beds. Joey and I bunk together, and I claim the top bunk. At my age how many more chances will I have to get the top bunk?

(Joke: People are always saying, "Hey, how is the weather up there?" I always want to bonk them on the head and say, "Hail the size of my fists.")

Chapter Twenty Eight

Our MWR contact opens the door with a flourish and loudly yells, "Rise and shine!" I'm grateful that I could not sleep last night, if only that I am essentially ready to roll. We pull ourselves together and head to base security where our passports and military orders are checked and we get photo IDs shot and fingerprints taken. Whenever you get a military identification, you always look half dead. That's because you are either rushed in five minutes after you wake up or after sixteen hours on a plane. I mention to Joey that since they have our prints on file we can no longer fall back on a career in crime. The longer I do comedy, the fewer options I have with the rest of my life.

We have already missed breakfast so decide to check out the PX while we wait for the dining facility to open. While looking around I see a Kuwaiti Harley Davidson T-shirt. I bet my brother-in-law would like it but I decide to wait and see if I can find one when we get to Iraq. Shortly thereafter, we hit the dining hall, where lunch is served to well over 2,000 soldiers. Once again, I note that the Army has got the skill of serving quality food quickly down to a science.

The next stop is at the MWR office to check our emails. One is from a guy who runs freedomphone.org, a nonprofit company that provides video phones to soldiers so they can see and talk to their loved ones. He has given me a list of bases in Iraq that he has gotten his equipment to. I have been talking to him via email about the possibility of broadcasting to the Jimmy Kimmel Show from Iraq, maybe getting some soldiers to tell jokes and say hello to loved ones. The problem is that I am only going to one base on his list and that trip is Sunday, a day they do not tape the Jimmy Kimmel Show. For security reasons, I really don't know how much of my schedule I should be emailing around. I will ask my point of contact, Lt. Col. Saunders, for his advice. I print out the email and decide after talking to the Lt. Col. Saunders to give it to our POC in Iraq to see if he can help with logistics. I think it's a long shot.

Our trip to Camp Patriot is about an hour and fifteen minutes long. Our Suburban cruises on these great freeways at about ninety miles per hour. Along the road you can see power plants, brand new buildings and sheepherders herding their flocks under high-tension wires. I see a bunch of camels, some of the most bizarre animals on earth. Someone said they look like God made them with the parts left over from all the other animals. We go through the gates and have our papers and IDs checked.

Our show time has been moved up from 8 p.m. to 6 p.m. Joey and I agree that this is a bad omen. Anytime a place changes the time and venue at the last moment, I'm afraid no one will be at the show. When we get to our venue we feel even more trepidation. It is a cafeteria with a set-up that might make it difficult for every-one to see us. One thing about doing these tours is that you have to make do with what you get, no matter how terrible or weird. A guitar amp will serve as our sound system tonight. Who says show business isn't glamorous? After a few minutes surveying the ven-ue, we decide to move all of the tables to one side of the room and arrange chairs on the other side of the room to create theater-style seating. Some soldiers pitch in and we get the chairs rearranged in no time.

Then we eat.

At 5:45 p.m. Joey and I are thinking this could be a very tough gig. There are only six people sitting in our makeshift theatre. It's Joey's turn to go first so he has it the worst. I can see in his face he is expecting to receive a beating.

I say "Joe, if it sucks go short on time. I'll try to make it up on the back end of the show after they have been warmed up a little."

At about 5:55 p.m. about ninety soldiers shuffle in and sit down. I bring Joey up to a warm round of applause. I can see in the first five minutes that instead of being the tough show that we both predicted, this show would be the most fun we have had so far. The audience is great. After the show, almost everyone gets in line to shake our hands, ask for autographs, and thank us for coming over. I tell them all with complete honesty that no one has more fun or gets more gratification at these shows than I do.

The MWR guy is from Hawaii. He asks me if I would like to do my act in Hawaii. I tell him, "Hell, yes."

You know, if I can't do every show in a cafeteria in the middle of the desert, Hawaii would be okay as a fallback.

After we return to our base, I have the opportunity to use a phone to call my mom and wish her a happy belated birthday. She asks me where I am. I tell her I am overseas. When she hears that, I know she thinks I'm in Europe, so I quickly change the subject. I do not want her to worry about me being in Iraq. I'll tell her when I get back, my feeling being that it's often better to beg for forgiveness than ask for permission.

Chapter Twenty Nine

Jim McCue & Casey Cmiel

Some Kuwaitis checking phone lines wake us. I check my email, where there is a message from my cousin Rick. It does not contain specific information about Casey's unit. Over breakfast I talk to a soldier who directs me to a military web page that has information about various locations.

Today we are going to Camp New York, and my meeting with Casey Cmiel.
We load our stuff into the Suburban. Our party consists of tour manager Jeff, Joey, me, and armed escorts LT. Col. Eddie Saunders and Capt. Zimmerman. Our driver's name is Brody. We take off on a two-hour journey, half of which is off road. About forty-five minutes into the trip we pass an expansive collection of burned-out and abandoned Iraqi vehicles and artillery piled up on each side of the road. This Iraqi equipment was abandoned during Desert Storm. I guess the Iraqi army did not have Triple-A.

As we continue on our journey we come upon a large group of camels crossing the road. Our escorts decide it is safe for us to get out and take some pictures. We all shuffle out of our tightly packed vehicle and start pulling out our cameras and video equipment. What appears to be the largest of the camels starts towards us. I think I can speak for all of us when I say that we initially think that this is a great chance for a close up, but that our thoughts on that change very quickly. The camel seems to be charging.

We all run for the Suburban in a panicked and undignified retreat. We are climbing over each other, seeking the safety of the vehicle. Brody starts to drive the vehicle away, nearly leaving Capt. Zimmerman behind. The captain deftly runs around to the other side of the vehicle.

The camel stops and looks us over. He concludes (correctly) that we are no threat to the herd. With a snort and a dirty look he continues across the street. We take more pictures, although this time from a distance, and continue on our journey. We are all in great spirits as we continue towards Camp New York, reliving our lack of bravery in the face of danger.

Camp New York is a huge, flat dustbowl situated in the middle of nowhere. Upon arrival we pass through the checkpoints and gates. Then we follow the bucket loader to the stage. We ask our POC (point of contact) where we'll be performing. He points at four flatbed trucks standing side-by-side.

"It's parked right over there," he says.

"How many soldiers are you expecting?"

"Maybe 3,000."

We start setting up our sound system -- which is fine for many areas but probably not for an open-air theater for 3,000 -- and a sand storm hits. With inadequate sound and tough weather, this should be a heckuva show, I think. As we set up our microphone and amplifiers, a soldier approaches.

"Hey Jim, your cousin is here."

The soldier is standing with another soldier, whose name patch reads Cmiel.

I climb down from the flatbed truck and give him a hug and a hello. I haven't seen Casey in ten years, and he looks very different to me. He's gotten husky, heavy even. He asks me about my mother and father and each of my brothers and sisters. I give him an update -- Mike is married with kids, John has a girlfriend, Helen is living in Boston, my nephew Jessie is in California -- but can't get over how much Casey has changed. I look into this stranger's face and wonder what kinds of experiences he has endured in Sadr City. Still, I am feeling a rush of joy that he's here, healthy.

He then steps out of character and says, "Guess what? I'm not Casey! He is!"

He points about twenty feet to my right, at another soldier. I have been the victim of a practical joke.

"Man," I say as the real Casey steps forward. "That was cold."

I am really embarrassed, made to be an ass in front of his friends.

Casey and I awkwardly replay the catch-up that I just had with the fake Casey. I tell Casey that the show is at seventeen hundred hours; maybe we can catch up for real afterwards. He says, "Sure," and he and his friend walk off laughing and clapping each other on the backs.

I am stung a little by the practical joke -- how much I was looking forward to catching up with him. Joey admits that it was a little weird, and I wonder if people ever go nuts when they get "punked" on TV. I guess that's what makes a practical joke funny, when the person watching gets to see you make an ass of yourself.

We decide to get something to eat at the dining facility. The wind has been picking up. I'm wearing goggles, but can still feel sand in my teeth and eyes. The sand in this region is fine to the touch, and a layer is covering my hair and face. Between the camel attack, the practical joke and the sand storm, the day -- and the trip -- is beginning to wear me down. I ask God to give me strength before I eat, and he does me one better. Our POC mentions over the meal that there is a tent we could use for the show. It can't fit 3,000, but I tell him Joey and I will do six shows if necessary if we can perform inside. After dinner, he brings us to a tent that can seat 500. It's perfect. We quickly move our sound system into the tent and post a couple of soldiers to tell everyone where the show has been moved to.

When 700 soldiers arrive, we fit them all in. Just before I bring up Joey, Casey appears and gives me a ceramic camel with which to remember my adventure. This is the kind of thoughtful person I remember, a kid who sent great "thank you" letters for care packages I had sent him in the past. I wonder if he realizes how awkward he had made me feel, and is trying to make amends. "Thank you -- you didn't have to," I say. If anyone knows what it's like to misfire with a joke, it's me. "Let's grab a cup of coffee after the show."

I step onto the stage to say a few words to start the show, and introduce Joey. As I do so, I am trying to figure out how I can carry a ceramic camel all over Iraq without breaking it. I also picture my girlfriend's face as she reacts to my suggestion to put the camel in her living room.

Joey crushes for the next forty minutes; then it's my turn. I have a red hot set filled with applause breaks and even a partial standing ovation. We are the first entertainers these soldiers have seen in a long time and they are eating it up. They have become very close and really enjoy my picking out their friends and having fun with their various jobs. I really feel honored to be included in this family of soldiers, if only for a couple of hours.

After the show Joey and I are signing for a long line of autograph seekers and Casey waits patiently. He even asks me for an autograph. I said, "Casey, we're family." He insists he wants an autograph and I give it to him, but I feel like it widens the gap between us. We get about ten-fifteen minutes to talk, and it feels good to me. It's good to see him, and I'm glad he's going home.

Chapter Thirty

Jim McCue & Joey Carroll prepare to board C-130

In our first day in Mosul, Iraq, we are pleasantly surprised to find a real, honest-to-goodness hard brick and mortar theater. This is where the soldiers in Camp Diamondback watch movies, at a place with real theater seats. It's perfect for a comedy show. It's my turn to go first, so Joey brings me up to the stage and we are off and running. The audience is a little stiff, but after a few minutes they get into the mood and the rest of the night is a ball. I do forty minutes, and Joey closes it out with a great set. After the show, a table is set up for Joey and me to sign autographs and meet and greet the soldiers. Then we go back to our trailer and sack out for the night.

But I don't sleep well. Our trailer is located close to where the planes and Black Hawks are landing. I keep thinking about the fact that this base has not been attacked with mortars or rockets and I wonder if we are overdue. I wonder what they would write in my obituary. "Among the fatalities in Iraq today was one American comedian. We've never heard of him. In other news, Ling Ling the Giant Panda has a hangnail... We'll take a closer look after this commercial break."

Chapter Thirty One

US Soldiers make the best audiences in the world

Joke: The male soldiers have a one to ten scale they use to rate how attractive the female soldiers are. Of course there are about 1,000 males for every female, so if you are in Iraq and you are a female you are a ten.

Joke: A lot of soldiers complain that they have not been with a woman because they have been deployed for a year. But I've met some of these guys, and I'm betting being deployed has got nothing to do with it.

It's a personality issue.

Chapter Thirty Two

Jim McCue & Bodyguard "Shadow JR"

It's my second day in Mosul, Iraq. I wake up early, grab my flashlight, find my shaving kit, towel and clean underwear. I make my way to the latrine and showers in the pitch black. I clean up, and as I walk back to my quarters run into a female soldier who is doing a video piece on Joey and me for the Pentagon Channel. I'd poked fun at her the night before, during the show.

We chat outside for a bit, talking about the weather and politics. She has been in the Army for quite some time, and we find that one thing we agree on is that the press back home never talks about all the wonderful things our military people do around the globe.

Slowly, others from our party join our conversation. First are the smokers, in need of their morning nicotine fix. At first light, Lt. Col. Saunders returns from his morning regimen and joins our group, which heads to the dining facility. Picking out my breakfast, I notice that an intense looking soldier with a semi-automatic machine gun is shadowing me. At first I don't think anything of it. Everyone has a weapon. When I stand to get sugar for my coffee, the soldier stands and follows. I turn to him and ask, "Are you with us?" meaning our group.

"Yes, sir," he responds.

"Are you protecting me?" I ask.

"Yes, sir."

"Did the show last night go that badly?"

"No, sir."

"You don't talk much."

"No, sir."

We finish breakfast without speaking, which is actually a pretty good arrangement, since I'm not much of a morning person. Our next stop is the helipad. We wait for a couple of hours for our ride to our first base. Five serious looking soldiers, one being the female with whom I had conversed with earlier that morning, join our party. While waiting, I tell our camel attack story and about some of our adventures in Kyrgyzstan and Bosnia. We hear some stories as well. A generator had been hit by a rocket last week and had produced a lot of black smoke.

In Vietnam, the Viet Cong were referred to as Charley. Here the local population is referred to as Hajji. So they have Hajji Shops, Hajji Armor, and Hajji Cokes.

We go to a Hajji shop. Given my height, the chances of me finding clothes that fit are slim to none, but maybe there will be something for my girlfriend. They have knockoff designer purses and pocketbooks. I decide not to buy anything for two reasons. First, I don't know the difference between a handbag worth buying and one not worth it. Second, I would not want to get hit by some stray mortar and all they send back to my family is my ID and my purse.

Our Black Hawk helicopters arrive at noon. We grab our luggage and pile in. This is my first ride in a Black Hawk. It has a pilot and what I think is a co-pilot. Two gunners sit behind the pilot facing out on the starboard and port sides. One is the crew chief, who is responsible for everything, including protecting the pilot, passengers and cargo. The ride is incredible. While planes fly, it is said that helicopters beat the air into submission. The Black Hawks fly in teams of at least two choppers. If one chopper is forced to land or crashes, the other can provide air support until help arrives. I expect to be scared out of my wits, but the flight is exhilarating. We travel about 100 feet off the ground, flying at 150 miles per hour. With the exception of a few banking maneuvers I feel fine. I learn really quickly to anticipate that roller coaster feeling as we are up and down over power lines.

The trip takes about thirty minutes. We arrive at Camp Q West. It is an air base formerly inhabited by Suddam Hussein's air force. According to my information, it features more than thirty three dispersed hardened aircraft shelters and once housed MiG 25s and 27s and M-1 Mirage fighters. MiG's are Russian built and the Mirage fighters are from France. Is it such a big surprise why they were against ousting Saddam Hussein?

(Joke: The French have the only fighter with built-in retreat controls).

We are met by a handful of people who usher us into vehicles. We are driven to a small brick building, which I assume is used for billeting. As we are ushered through the building we find many smiling faces and outstretched hands, and arrive at a meeting room where we are greeted by a nice fruit, cheese and cracker platter. On a dry board it says "Welcome Jim and Joey from Laugh Force." They have put some effort into making us feel welcome, and it works.

We shake hands and thank everyone for their sacrifices, and are shown our performance space. We walk outside, across the semi-paved road to what looks like a drive-in. This is an outdoor theater Hussein had designed for his airmen to watch movies in, but the set-up is all wrong for a live show. The ground is muddy and wet, and there is no real sound system. My tour manager Jeff turns to me and says, "Well, Jim, this is on you."

So much for being spoiled by our first tour manager.

I sheepishly ask if there is an inside venue in case it rains. I'm told sure, they have a theater at their MWR facility and I say it would be great if we could perform there. Here is the surprising part. The officer says, "You want to be inside? No problem." He posts a man to tell the soldiers the show will be held at the MWR facility. This is remarkable. Only in the military could you move a show strictly by word of mouth one hour before show time and have the audience find you.

Within an hour we are moved inside to a beautiful indoor theater, which doubles as a movie theater and chapel. The sound and light systems aren't great, but the show goes well.

Afterwards, a colonel presents us with memento coins from his unit. These coins are beautiful and each one is unique. They vary from the size of a silver dollar to about twice that size. Some are made of bronze and some of silver. Military challenge coins are also known as military coins, unit coins. The coins represent each unit.

They are each engraved with the insignia motto and other markings unique to the unit history of the unit that had them cast. It is a huge honor to receive them. I wish I had a coin to give these brave men and women.

Joey and I sign some autographs. As we sign, our bodyguards stand watch. I haven't quite gotten used to it, but a personal bodyguard protects every person in our party. Mine is the guy I met during breakfast. These are the same bodyguards that protected Vice President Cheney on his last visit. That makes me feel very important. I bet they won't tell him the same group that guarded the comedians protected him.

Joey and I sign autographs and pose for pictures, one of which I take with my bodyguard. That's not for him, but for me, because otherwise no one would believe it. Finally it is time for us to catch our helicopter to the next base. At the heliport, some of the staff gives us souvenir Iraqi money and we take some final pictures. We get on the Black Hawk and are off again.

Chapter Thirty Three

Jim McCue & Joey Carroll

Our escorts travel with us on another exhilarating ride, this time partly traveling along the Tigress River. It ends at a palace.

This was once the palace of Suddam's son Uday. It is also the home base for our security force, whose members are friendly with several soldiers at this base. Once again we pile into a couple of SUVs with all of our gear. The first stop is the latrine for Joey.

We learn later that the lieutenant colonel has sent word ahead that Joey likes Diet Coke so every time we arrive at a new base, the first thing they are sure to do is to hand Joey a couple of Diet Cokes. Not wanting to seem unappreciative, Joey thanks them and promptly drinks one, resulting in the latrine stops.

We meet with a general who now has his office located at Uday's palace. We are ushered through checkpoints where our IDs are checked. Our armed guards, led by an affable captain, vouch for us. Then we are whisked up the stairs past more guards into an office where our paperwork is checked once again. We are told to step into the next room and that the general will meet with us in a moment. Our security force, with the exception of the captain, is asked to wait outside. Our bodyguards seem concerned to let us out of their sight, even for a moment, even in this secure environment. We are led into a big room. We could easily do a show in here for 200 people. There is a large leather couch and some other furniture that I think was left from its previous inhabitant. As we wait, I am blown away that I'm sitting in the palace of a fallen psychopath, waiting to meet a general.

We hear gunfire and an explosion, but I don't feel afraid. It just seems unreal to me. Joey springs up and runs to the window to see where the gunfire is coming from. I laugh and say that maybe standing next to the window is not the best place to be when there is gunfire. We all laugh. I am relieved to see him return and flop down on one of the couches. Feeling like a mother hen, I tell Joey, "Sit up; we're meeting a general, not getting ready to watch The Simpsons." He corrects his posture and an officer comes in and apologizes. The general is tied up in a meeting. We all agree that if meeting comedians is on the top of his to-do list, we are all in trouble.

A few moments later the general arrives. We all jump to our feet, and he graciously shakes our hands and asks us to sit. He thanks us for coming over to boost morale. The general tells us that the tide is turning here. There is a lot of work to be done, he says, but the people of Iraq want to be free. He says that our troops are working closely with Iraqi troops and police to turn over protection of Iraq to a newly elected Iraqi government. He apologizes for having to cut our meeting short; he is headed to a memorial service for one of his men. He thanks us again, turns to our captain and says, "If anything happens to these comedians, it's your ass."

When the general leaves, I tell the captain, "Relax. What's the worst thing they can do to you, shave your head and send you to Iraq?"

He smiles, but shoots me a look that tells me there are always worse things you can be doing.

Before the show, we tour the palace-turned-base. There is a small PX, a large room turned into a weight training facility, and a beautiful house on a man-made pond that now serves as the general's quarters. The house and pond are surrounded by lush green lawn and plant life. We are here during the winter and all of the plants are getting plenty of rain. It must be a good deal less green when the 130 degree days arrive in July. I would not want to be one of these soldiers sporting forty-five pounds of body armor and a helmet and weapon when it gets that hot.

As we walk around the palace, our bodyguards abruptly stop us. There is a crowd gathered around the pool house, which is the venue where they'd planned to do our show. The bodyguards don't like the look of it. One is sent to investigate. He promptly returns, and tells us that they are having the venue searched by bomb-sniffing dogs.

I try to push the idea of bombing literally out of my head.

I'm glad to see the dogs. I'm a big animal lover, although I know this is not the kind of dog you pet unless you want to be called lefty for the rest of your life.

In another area of the pool house, which is now used for weight training, our guide shows us a crude blueprint gouged on the wall. He explains that Saddam Hussein was not happy with the first two architects, so he executed them. The third architect asked Hussein to please show him what he envisioned, so Hussein gouged a crude blueprint into the marble wall with a screwdriver and scratched his signature. The third architect was not murdered. This was definitely not a union job.

As we walk deeper into the palace there is a marble staircase that rises both to the left and to the right. There are huge tile murals of Saddam Hussein, including one with a young girl, who even in her tile likeness looks terrified. The other image is of Saddam patting a woman's burka on her head. This is not a picture of womanhood that Jane Fonda would approve of.

While we tour the palace we note that even though there is a great deal of intricate workmanship with wood, tile and marble, upon close inspection much of the work is shoddy. Similar to Las Vegas, some of the buildings look grand, but up close they might look a little less impressive, maybe cheesy.

Our new friend, the captain, says their dining facility has the best food in Iraq. We find the food in most of the bases to be quite good, and are also aware that every base makes the same claim to having the best food. I figure it is a good problem.

Inside the dining hall; the large room has been divided by sandbag-filled walls so that the groups of men eating in any segment are kept small. I realize this is a result of the bombing of the dining facility that killed and wounded so many soldiers. These walls will reduce the amount of casualties if such an attack is repeated. The thought is quite sobering. After we eat, we have an hour to shower and shave before tonight's performance.

When we arrive at what was Uday's pool house, the room is set up great, thanks to our friend from MWR. A new challenge arises when we are informed that due to security concerns, the posters advertising the show do not divulge the date, time, or place of our show. Only the military could conceive of putting on a show and for security reasons not tell anyone where, when, or who is in the show.

However, if there is one thing I've learned from these bases, it's that word of mouth travels fast and that everyone eats at the dining facility. After some rushed printing of new flyers that feature the: who, what and where, we get a few volunteer soldiers to head over to the dining facility and tell everyone about our show, which starts in less than an hour.

Two by two and four by four, the pool house begins to fill up with soldiers. The room is about two-thirds full when I take the stage.

A huge man who works for Halliburton is sitting with a friend in the front row. He is wearing a bright Hawaiian shirt and his feet are propped up on the stage. His posture signals an obvious challenge to the comedians. I take the stage. Almost immediately he yells something out. I don't panic. This is what I trained for. What this guy doesn't realize is that I'm a comedian who does a lot of crowd work. I'm not going to be thrown by some heckler. I do my act hundreds of times a year under all kinds of conditions. He has not.

I ask him what he does for a living and he tells me that he works for Halliburton. I said "Oh so you don't do anything."

Big laugh accompanied by a round of applause.

I have another advantage tonight. Stage left and right are the bodyguards assigned to protect us, standing there with their automatic weapons, and a full clip in the gun. I point them out and tell the crowd that they get to go home early if they shoot someone from Halliburton and reduce the national deficit by a million dollars.

This draws another big laugh, and more applause.

My large friend trades some more quips with me, but you can tell he just wants to get off this ride without losing face. So that's what I do. I ask everyone to give him a round of applause for being a good sport. They do and now I am free to continue the show. My large heckling friend will not shout any more, and he settles in to laugh and enjoy the show.

The rest of it goes great. By the time I'm ready to bring out Joey, the room is full and the crowd is warmed up. My work is done. Joey goes up and closes it out. After the show, we sign a bunch of autographs.

We grab some food and head back to our sleeping quarters. Tonight, we're sleeping in a trailer.

Many of the soldiers live in small trailers also. Which leads me to a joke I use in camps similar to this one.

"How many people grew up in trailer parks?" I ask, a question that always brings some acknowledgement from the audience.

"And you thought, "I have to get out of here. I'm not going to spend the rest of my life in a trailer park. I'm going to join the Army,'" I say. "Then you get here and they show you where you are going to live and you say to yourself... 'Crap!'"

Chapter Thirty Four

Jim McCue, poses with captured Iraqi Jet.

Joke: The first Iraqi elections had to be the strangest elections anywhere.

Iraqi Mayoral candidate: "Psssst…. Hey… I'm running for mayor... Don't tell anyone."

Chapter Thiry Five

Uday's Palace

I wake to a clock alarm, reach over and tap it silent. It is pitch-black. Someone's watch alarm sounds. Our entire party groans. Bone-tired, we bitch and moan as everyone crawls out of bed. There are a bunch of us, sleeping in bunks in a trailer. Jeff is trying to scrounge twenty extra winks as I shower and shave. There is a spider that has made a home in the sink -- one nasty looking customer. I decide this is one insurgent I'm not going to mess with. Instead, I pack up my toiletries and beat a hasty retreat from the bathroom.

On this trip, much of our time and effort is spent packing and unpacking our clothes, and some items always get left behind. (The last twenty days, we've slept in more beds than Paris Hilton. I'll be here all week. Try the veal.)

We go to the dining facility and I grab some coffee and pancakes from the chow line. When I sit down, I realize I forgot the sugar for my coffee. I stand and walk to get some and my armed escort springs up behind me.

"Relax. I'm just getting some sugar."

"Let's get it together, sir."

I stand there in disbelief.

"I can get your sugar if you'll stay with the other escorts, sir."

I laugh. It's been a few days, but this bodyguard thing is still not sinking in with me.

"No," I say, "Let's get it together. And while we're over there we can talk about our feelings."

I manage to draw a smile, but still no laugh. The guy is a heck of a bodyguard but as an audience member he's tough. I've made it my goal to elicit laughter from him, but for now decide that early morning is a tough time to do stand-up.

He's a good guy, though. He allows me to call my girlfriend Bernadette on his satellite phone. There is some gunfire at a shooting range near where we are standing. I'm afraid she will hear it, but she doesn't. It is difficult to talk all lovey-dovey to your girl when you have an armed soldier in body armor standing just three feet away. Next, I call my parents. I get their answering machine, so hang up.

We finish our breakfast and go to the helipad. We wait on the helipad for a couple of hours, with our luggage and body armor. There are Black Hawks sitting there, but they do not appear to be going anywhere. This business of hurry-up and wait is a recurring theme while entertaining the troops, especially if you are waiting for a Black Hawk, which is the Army's workhorse.

We understand the aircraft probably have much more important things to do than haul comedians around, which does not stop us from speculating on the well-known fact that cheerleaders rarely wait for helicopters. I wish I still had my girlish figure.

The sound of gunfire rings from a gate about 200 yards away. Our escorts draw their weapons and step in front of us. It seems reflexive. Then they relax and go back to talking.

I say to my bodyguard, "So you're my bodyguard."

"Yes sir."

"You still don't talk much"

"No Sir."

"OK... Well, maybe we should just rest your vocal cords."

This line draws a smirk. From this guy, it's like a standing ovation. I couldn't have been happier if he'd been in the front row at a comedy club and I'd made him spit beer through his nose. But as odd as it felt, I appreciated his efforts.

We left him in Mosul, and I never got his name or hometown. Maybe he was shy, and maybe a little afraid that anything he said could and would be used against him in my stand-up act.

Chapter Thirty Six

Jim McCue & Joey Carroll

After a few hours at the helipad, our captain returns and sends us back to our trailer. He'll find out what is happening with our transportation. We go back to our trailer and I fall asleep instantly. Twelve minutes later a soldier slaps me on the feet and says, "Let's roll. The helicopter is here."

Everything is packed, and we're into the SUV. At the helipad, with the Black Hawk blades whirling, we trade handshakes, pats on the back, and hand gestures with our armed escorts, a quick goodbye. During our couple of days going from base to base in Mosul these men have become a part of our group. I really cannot tell you how quickly you bond with our people over here. For some reason, we always expect to have a few moments to have a few words with the friends we meet from the bases, but most often it ends with a few hurried words that may be drowned out by the roar of aircraft engines. This is what I think as we lift off in our helicopter, as they wait on the ground, their mission completed.

On our flight, despite the constant noise, Joey and the rest of our party took catnaps. I could not close my eyes. I did not want to miss one moment of the ride. As we soared over the countryside, I still had that image of pulling up, away from our bodyguards. As ludicrous as it seemed to me, these soldiers took the duty so seriously, it was clear to me that they put our safety before their own. What guts, I thought, and not something that a simple "thank you" will cover. One of them told me that being assigned to protect us was an honor. He really should look that word up in a dictionary, I thought. He might find a picture of himself.

I know that being in the company of these great Americans, the honor was all mine.

As our next leg of the tour begins, our destination is Tikrit, and Camp Speicher. Once again the Black Hawk ride is exhilarating. We are packed in with soldiers, our luggage thrown upon our laps. We had been told that these helicopters are workhorses not designed for comfort, and they don't disappoint in that regard. Still, the view is spectacular. We fly over sod homes and herds of sheep, and I wonder what these farmers think of us. Many of them smile and wave. I take that as a good sign.

We were all feeling pretty tired. Lt. Col. Saunders and Joey both fell asleep on the Black Hawk, which is no easy task; 150 feet off the ground, thumping along at 150 miles an hour. As our flight draws closer to Tikrit it begins to rain. By the time our Black Hawk touches down it is pouring.

Chapter Thirty Seven

Jim McCue & Captain Condon

Coalition forces' only air-to-air loss during the 1991 Gulf War was the plane of Navy Cmdr. Michael Scott Speicher, who was shot down over Iraq on the opening night of the Gulf War on January 17, 1991. He was originally considered "killed in action, body not recovered." Iraqi authorities provided a small amount of human remains they claimed to be those of Speicher. U.S. military experts determined this to be untrue. Iraq later claimed that animals devoured his body and no remains were found. At first, it was believed that Speicher had been killed in action. But later, evidence found at the crash site and reports from Iraqi defectors and foreign intelligence services indicated that Speicher had survived the crash and was a prisoner of war in Iraq.

Of course I know none of this when we land.

This is not the first base that does not have someone to greet us at the helipad, just the first one today. We schlep our gear 100 yards while wearing forty-five pounds of body armor. We are soaked and tired as Lt. Col. Saunders leads us into a tent, which passes for a Blackhawk ticket counter. An attractive female soldier asks us to follow her to the MWR tent. This tent has a television and about sixty seats.

Joey is exhausted and a little cranky. When miserable, tired and cranky, Joey is at his funniest. He is about a foot shorter and 100 pounds lighter than me, but always threatens my life in some new creative way, like he's going to hit me in the face with a coal shovel or bash my head in with a ball-peen hammer. I generally respond to the threat by congratulating him on his originality and we both laugh.

The tent is empty. Joey falls asleep sitting up. I decide to leave him alone this time. I hook my camera up to the TV and Jeff and I watch some of our recent adventures. In the absence of DVDs or cable, it's the only game in town.

After we watch a few tapes and run out of remarks about my horrible skills as a cameraman, Lt. Col. Saunders decides to find out what happened to our welcoming committee. I cannot express how valuable Lt. Col. Saunders has been in getting this tour to work successfully. His efforts have been tireless in getting us set up in as good a venue as possible and into the best quarters available. Many times he is the last to bed and the first one on his feet. Jeff decides to take a smoke break and I decide to find the location of the nearest latrine. As a general rule for these tours, whenever you get the chance to use the latrine, I suggest you take it.

The pouring has stopped and although there are puddles big enough to float a fishing trawler, I decide to walk around and shoot some more unwatchable videos. While I hop around in a vain attempt to keep my boots dry, I take some footage of what I perceive to be the smallest base we have worked on thus far. Then I spy Lt. Col. Saunders being led by a female captain and about three soldiers. I follow them to the tent. By the time I catch up with them the soldiers are already carrying my luggage and following the captain. She mistakes our tour manager for one of the comedians. I guess she figured I was the tour manager. "Wait until she sees him perform," I think to myself. As we pile into the vehicles, Lt.

Col. Saunders generously offers me the front seat for the rest of the journey.

As we leave the helipad I realize what I originally thought to be a small base was only the support tents and building for one helipad. The base is huge. I am also wrong about our loss of celebrity status. Capt. Liz Condon heads our welcoming committee. She and our group had been waiting on the helipad for hours. They just ducked into a tent during the downpour and missed us sneaking in during the downpour. She welcomes us to the base and tells us what to do in case of a mortar or rocket attack. We are to go into a bunker and wait until at least thirty minutes after the last blast before coming out. This is good synergy, because to lie down like a slug is my natural defense mechanism.

On the paved road leading to our quarters we see buildings rebuilt to military code, though with the spray of bullet holes and bomb damage still apparent. Camp Speicher is located near Tikrit, which is Suddam Hussein's home town. Something tells me he will not be available for his next class reunion. As we tour the camp we see a large portrait of him on a concrete wall. Soldiers had shot out his eyes, and someone had painted in pupils that make him look comically cross-eyed.

Camp Speicher is responsible for controlling the supply for food, medicine, maintenance and fuel in the region. Capt. Condon told us about her mission to go out to local schools providing shoes and pants to the children. The soldiers also give out candy, and have learned that the local children have a love for Beanie Babies.

We went to the dynamic stadium. I'm not sure if this is the proper name or a description. It had been bombed. Capt. Condon told us we would not be able to perform at the stadium because of the rain. I was glad we were being moved inside, rain or shine. Stand-up comedy is an indoor sport.

Capt. Condon then brought us to our quarters. We were surprised and delighted to find the best quarters of our entire tour. The building had large bunk beds with real mattresses and comforters, indoor bathrooms with showers and toilets. "If we are going to get stuck anywhere on the trip, let it be here," I thought. "With a real bed and indoor plumbing."

The captain and her company had put a great deal of care into the fruit baskets with chips and treats for each of us. The building was large enough so we could spread out into three rooms. Joey and I took one and Lt. Col. Saunders and Jeff each took one. That left one room in case a female checked in so she could have some privacy. There is a metal staircase that led to the roof. I go up there and am able to survey the buildings and fields surrounding our quarters. I can see a berm, which is a wall of dirt piled up around a base. They are common at these bases. I estimate this one to be about eight feet high. Outside of the berm is a vehicle riddled with bullet holes. I could only speculate what bit of history it might have played a part in. There are rows of tents in which soldiers were probably sleeping; quarters that I suspect are much less comfortable than our own.

I make my way back into our room. Joey and I would not have been happier if we found ourselves at Disney World. We talk to Lt. Col. Saunders and Capt. Condon about our schedule and agree we would like to trade dinner for three hours of sleep. The heat is not working, but I don't mind. I am fast asleep within minutes, my final thought before slipping away to thank God for the comfortable bed. About two and a half hours later, we are awoken.

My father does this, I realize. If you say, "I'm getting up at 9:00 a.m." he will wake you up at 8:30 to make sure you are awake by 9. I suddenly suspect he picked this habit up in the marines.

We shower and shave in about twenty minutes. We walk from our safe, comfortable hardened building to the theater, which is a movie theater with a perfect set up for comedy. I wonder if Saddam and his men ever watched The Three Stooges here.

Joey and I hurriedly set up our video cameras. As we discuss how we should start the show, someone barks, "Ten hut!" Everyone jumps to his or her feet as General Sullivan takes the stage. He is a rather soft-spoken man -- when you're a general, people better develop their listening skills -- and said some very nice things about me, and the fact that I chose to be here and that I grew up in West Hartford. I guess he went to my website, or had someone research it for him. Then he invited me to come on stage.

Well it was Joey's turn to go first, but when a general invites you on stage, you're on! I reach the stage, and he shakes my hand and places a large coin in it. I have been given coins before, once from Gen. Wesley Clark, so I knew what it was. Soldiers receive these coins as a reward and not every soldier gets one, especially from a general. I received coins from ten different bases on this trip, and it sounds quaint, but I treasure every one of them. It's a big honor.

I bring Joey up and he does forty-five minutes and sets a dubious new comedy record. During his set, three microphones break. Have you heard of Murphy's Law, that anything that can go wrong will? Joey's version is, "Anything that can go wrong, will go wrong while Joey Carroll is on stage."

Still, nothing throws him. He has as strong a set as he can, given the interruptions, and I follow with a forty-five minute set with no microphone problems. Then, we reverse our order and do a second show. Both crowds are great. We check our emails and I receive word that, for a variety of logistical reasons, any hope I have of broadcasting to Jimmie Kimmel's show are pretty much shot in the ass. Capt. Condon, Lt. Col. Saunders and I take a break and enjoy a couple of cigars. I notice tables with various items people have sent to support our troops. It's nice to see people back home showing their support.

Chapter Thirty Eight

Col. Vicci & Joey Carroll

Eight a.m. comes way too early. We are all very comfortable in our quarters, and six hours does not seem like enough sleep, but we jump into our hot showers and get ready. We had eaten at midnight at the dining facility so don't eat breakfast, but do scrounge up some food out of the wonderful fruit baskets that were provided for us.

We arrive at Camp Danger around 11 a.m. Joey's friend, Col. Vicci met our Black Hawk. Before our trip, Joe was performing in Princeton, New Jersey, at a comedy club called Catch a Rising Star. Joey does a bit in his act about how he had met some Black Hawk pilots who were stuffing teddy bears with candy and dropping them to the children below. He talks about how the soldiers say it's no big deal. When he returned from his tour he saw actress Susan Sarandon and filmmaker Michael Moore bad-mouthing the war and thought those individuals don't support our troops. He says he would like to stuff them full of candy and drop them out of the airplanes. This usually gets a round of applause. He then mentions he would leave off the parachutes. He says the fun part would be watching the children beat them with sticks to get at the free candy.

Col. Vicci and some of his crew introduced themselves after the show in New Jersey. Joey mentioned that he would be touring Iraq, and Col. Vicci was just about to rotate over. They kept in touch via email until today.

Needless to say they are both pleased about the reunion. After some hugs and hellos, Col. Vicci offers to get us some coffee and give us a tour at Camp Danger. He gives us a drive-by tour of one of Saddam's retirement palaces. It is empty. Obviously, Saddam is not home.

The dome has a big hole, left by a U.S. rocket. I think this might have been the first shot fired in the war. We hit this palace hoping to take out Saddam with the first punch. He was not in, but we gave him a new skylight.

Our next stop was the palace of Saddam's mother. It makes me feel a little guilty that a scumbag like Saddam built his mom a palace and I have yet to buy my mother a birthday gift.

The palace is beautiful. There is a gym and a chapel. I'm sure there are offices, but we don't get to see any of them. From an outside deck built with marble and pillars, we can see the outer wall, which marks the perimeter of the base. Col. Vicci says rather casually that mortars are frequently launched at this palace from nearby buildings. I hope today is their day off.

We all pile into the hummer and head for the helicopter pad. When we arrive, Lt. Col. Saunders and the Black Hawk crew members are waiting for us. We have spent about an hour at Camp Danger, but it was great to see the palaces and for Joey to reunite with Col. Vicci.

Our next destination is FOB (Forward Operating Base) Warhorse, site of this afternoon's show. We seem to hop from base to base, picking up and dropping off soldiers. These Blackhawk crews really are vital to operations here. The trip is supposed to take twenty minutes but we arrive at Baqubah, Iraq Camp Warhorse about four and a half hours later. We have bounced from base to base bringing soldiers and supplies all over the area. Our point of contact, Capt. Jordan, meets us and brings us straight to where we are to perform our first show.

It is pouring rain as we pull up to a huge airplane hanger. Two things you don't expect when traveling to Iraq is cold and rain. It's like going to Florida and packing for a snowstorm.

There are about three seats set up in a hanger that could easily hold 5,000. This time it is Joey's turn to go first. With all the spectators standing, this is the worst kind of set up for stand-up comedy. Joey is a pro and he once again makes lemonade out of lemons. I have a lot of comedians ask me how to find work entertaining the troops and a big part of it is working in situations that are less then perfect. No matter what the situation, you need to keep in mind that it is not about the performer, it's about the men and women in uniform who tough it out for us every day.

The best description I can give you of the show is that it goes off like we're doing comedy in an airplane hanger. The troops are wet from the rain and they're standing and the lights and acoustics are less than perfect, but we do the best we can. Because Joey and I are with the first group of entertainers, many of the folks who run these events at the different camps are still figuring out where to best put the shows. It's a trend that continues throughout our tour, but we will adapt and overcome because that's the mission.

The MWR official asks us to sign autographs. To our mutual surprise, a vast majority of the soldiers line up to meet us. They shake our hands, thank us for coming to Iraq and ask for our autographs. Apparently, they all had as much fun as 200 soldiers in forty-five pounds of wet body armor can have in an airplane hanger in Iraq.

When my father was a kid he fell down and almost poked hi eye out with a stick. For some reason, I think of that. Perhaps I'm guessing that our show this afternoon was better than a stick in the eye.

Chapter Thirty Nine

Jim McCue in a Bunker.

After the show, we are driven to our quarters. The base is muddy and it's difficult to walk. Apparently they have two seasons in Iraq; dust and mud. We are now enjoying the mud season. I am glad for my boots, because I would have lost a shoe in that crud for sure. Our quarters are trailers that barely fit two single beds. It must have been recently vacated because there is still a half-inch of mud on the floor from the previous inhabitants.

The mud makes our life interesting, because in order to change our clothes we have to keep our feet from touching the floor. We take cold showers, then head back to the dining facility to put on the feedbag. The food is good and the company even better. It never fails to give you a second wind when you look around and realize that you are just passing through and the people around you are putting up with more then just muddy boots and cold showers.

By the time we finish eating and walk out of the dining facility, it is pitch black. We are driven to a theater for our 7 p.m. show. The theater set up was perfect, with the seats close to the stage in nice neat rows. The rows are one higher then the other so every seat has a good view of the stage. It is built out of wood and sits about 400 soldiers.

I go up first and do my best to warm up the soldiers. My "trailer park" joke gets a good laugh. Joey closes, and predictably does a great job. We are both given coins for our service and for showing up. We sign some more autographs and get to meet and shake the hands of the good folks of FOB Warhorse. Capt. Jordan graciously lets us into his office to check our emails. We return home to our muddy trailer about 11:30 p.m. and I am asleep before my head hits the pillow.

Chapter Forty

Joey Carroll, Lt. Col. Saunder & Jim McCue catch forty winks.

We wake up around 7 a.m., eat and head to the helipad. We find ourselves waiting for a Blackhawk with some mercenaries and an independent reporter. The reporter's name is Michael Yon. He writes an online blog and shot a picture of a soldier cradling an Iraqi baby for which he was nominated for an award from Time Magazine. He has been in Iraq for some time. He is a really interesting, brave guy who actually goes out on fire missions with our troops.

While we are standing there, we hear gunfire in the distance. It is odd that we don't react, except to pause in our conversation, then continue. We've heard shots before, so when it happens now I reactively look to the soldiers. If they seem calm, it makes me feel calm. Monkey see, monkey do.

In the distance, I watch a small unit of soldiers cross the street in crouched postures. We hear some more shots... then nothing.

One of the soldiers tells us that once last week, the insurgents took pot shots at the guard towers. Nothing else happens.

We continue to talk, about last night's show, the war, and our backgrounds. Michael is a colorful guy who had also researched a book on cannibalism.

The temperature is cool, but Lt. Col. Saunders makes the best of our down time by laying out his body armor and catching a nap in the sun. It is not long before Joey and I follow his lead. I nod off until someone yells "Helicopters!" We jump up nearly simultaneously, and grab our gear. Moments later we are in a Black Hawk departing Baqubah, Iraq, FOB Warhorse.

Chapter Forty One

Jim McCue admiring F16

We arrive at noon at Balad, Iraq FOB Anaconda. This is one huge base. From the air we cannot see much more than the airport and the helipad we land on. There were rows of Chinooks helicopters, which are much bigger than Blackhawks. I wish I had better knowledge about the types of aircraft that are taking off and landing all around us. Suffice to say, it is one big mother of a place.

As we run from the helicopters and manage a thumbs-up to the crews, I try to keep my head down. I know intellectually that the blades won't chop my head off, but my mind's eye keeps picturing that blade lopping off the top of my head.

We reach what I consider a safe distance from the Black Hawks and are greeted by Capt. Hermesch and Capt. Chris Zimmerman, along with an MWR representative, Guy Donnie. As we are directed to a bus, we run into Captain Zimmerman. He is heading to FOB Warhorse. He is a sight for sore eyes. A unique type of bond happens between men when you have been chased like schoolgirls into a Suburban by camels in the Kuwait desert.

If you haven't lived through it, I don't expect you to understand.

Captain Zimmerman has been assigned the dangerous duty of escorting the group called the Perfect Angels, a group of professional cheerleaders. When it comes to the troops, this is the very top of the entertainment food chain. These are the same cheerleaders that we came into Kuwait with. There is a rumor that one of these ladies was featured in Playboy. I heard one soldier announce that they were not his type. Apparently denial is a river that runs through not only Egypt, but also Iraq.

The Angels looked tired as they shuffled past us, but they were troopers. They kept stopping every couple of feet to take pictures, and kept their smiles on. As each woman walked by, they politely said, "Hi," then walked out to the waiting choppers. As I have noted before, when cheerleaders are on military tours, there is always someone available to carry their bags, and there are always Black Hawks available. I believe that, in this regard, cheerleaders may outrank generals.

Capt. Zimmerman said goodbye, and we waited with our people until the Black Hawk flew out of site. You must wait, in the event the force of the wind, generated by the whirling blades, blows off the cheerleaders' clothes. You do not want to miss that.

As we ate lunch, our escorts inform us that we would be performing in the cafeteria shortly after we finish. This facility is about the size of a football field, with large-screen televisions along the outside walls. The television screens served to divide the room, as soldiers faced every which way, watching whatever caught their interest.

The tables are also arranged in a manner that assured that at least half of the soldiers will be completely blind sided by our impromptu performance. They are sitting around talking and have no idea that a show was scheduled. It is the worst possible layout for a show. Captain Hermesh informs us that we will be performing, and right now.

"What?" I think, as I stand rather awkwardly and walk over to the mike stand. This is an order, and this is our mission, but what a terrible idea.

"Hello everyone," I say, a statement that barely captures any attention from the soldiers. Except for one, who comes over and asks me very politely if I will sit down so he can watch the basketball game on the television behind me.

"No problem," I tell him. Then, into the mike, I introduce myself and tell the guys that we'll be performing tonight at the theater and "Enjoy the game."

I've just disobeyed a direct order, but you need to have guts to be in show business. Besides, I'm a civilian. What was he going to do, send me to Iraq?

I can see our escort does not approve of my choice to sit back down, but I did not come here to force myself on soldiers who want to relax and enjoy the game during their lunch break.

Plus, we had been wearing these sets of clothes for two days now, so we are anxious to get showered and into some clean clothes. We were told to put all our clothes into a laundry bag, because Lt. Col. Saunders had pulled some strings to get our laundry cleaned. All Joey and I had left was a pair of shorts and a couple of grey Boston Comedy Festival T-shirts, which we are wearing. We look like a couple of geeks, but our embarrassment would be easily cured by a hot shower and some clean clothes.

We are a little surprised to find that we are not going to our quarters, but to meet with some airmen who are busy armoring the hummers and trucks. They are working in a huge hanger. They are good guys, and one of them happily demonstrates how armoring had evolved in just a few years, since the beginning of the war. They line the vehicles up to illustrate how each is better protected than the model before it. The soldier stresses that almost all the vehicles were now armored. As we talk with all of the soldiers, we notice the pride in their voices as they describe the important work they do. We pile into the bus figuring we are heading to our quarters, but after a short drive we found ourselves outside a hanger with an F16 parked inside. Capt. Hermesh informs us that we are scheduled to meet the folks that maintain the aircraft. Before we go in, we need to wait as they decided whether to allow us in with our cameras. They didn't want us to inadvertently capture any military secrets.

While we were waiting, we walked over to an Iraqi jet in an

obvious state of disrepair. Soldiers had spray-painted graffiti all over it. We took some pictures. You can never have enough pictures with jets.

As we wait for approval to enter the hangar to see the F16, we are escorted by two airmen who take the time to explain their job -- loading ordnance (bombs) onto jets. Loading ordnance (bombs) is not a good job if you have the shakes. Joey, our tour manager Jeff, and   I each took turns signing a 500-pound bomb. I wish I had thought of something funny to write on it. But all I could think to write was "Eat Me." When in doubt, use a quote from Animal House.

After our education on smart bombs and dumb bombs we are taken into the hangar to meet the crew that maintains the Aircraft at FOB Anaconda. These people are very impressive, which makes me feel all the dorkier in my shorts and T-shirt.

Chapter Forty Two

Can you find the two civilians in this picture?

I have heard grumbling from some female soldiers that if the men get to see cheerleaders then the women should get to see Chippendales Dancers. I politely disagree. In the service, men outnumber women about One Thousand to One. If a female soldier wants to see a man dance naked, all she has to do is ask.

Besides, if the Army started flying in male strippers, there'd be less work for comedians.

Chapter Forty Three

Jim McCue with the Predator

Later that day, we are introduced to The Predator, an aircraft that looks like something you put together with your dad in the garage on weekends. What it can do is remarkable.

The Predator is an unmanned aircraft that can observe action on the ground from miles away, with incredible detail. How much detail? This thing can fly over an area, find two grasshoppers humping, and tell if one of them fakes an orgasm.

Takeoffs and landings are controlled via a setup that resembles an entire cockpit built into a suitcase, or the control box for a really cool video game. Because of the portability, the Predator can be piloted from just about anywhere. Forget what you saw in Top Gun. With this aircraft, a Las Vegas tourist in a Hawaiian shirt can fly a mission between sips of his Mai Tai.

We are suitably impressed with this show-and-tell, and then it's off to the MWR facility to perform our afternoon show. We have a blast, and return to our sleeping quarters to discover a minor military miracle: clean laundry.

Better still, we discover that our sleeping quarters will be top-notch -- separate rooms with a connecting bathroom. (Here's a tip for those considering a career in the military: the sleeping quarters are always the best on Air Force bases.) At this point in the trip, we look at beds the way soldiers look at cheerleaders.

We decide to skip dinner in exchange for three-hour naps, and within seconds I am on the bed and out.

Ten minutes later, I am pulled out of my REM sleep by the sound of Joey pounding on my door. The drain in the floor of the bathroom is churning up some nasty backwash at an alarming rate. Within moments our rooms are flooded and we are rushing to grab our belongings off of the floor.

We narrowly escape Saddam's backwash and walk half a block to the Air Force version of the concierge's desk. The frustration from the sewage attack is outweighed by our elation that we were able to salvage our clean underwear.

We get new digs, never get back to that nap, and a couple of hours later are showered and headed to the next gig. I'm a little beat and tired, but my underwear is clean and fresh.

This show takes place in a theater that Saddam was nice enough to build for us. The place is packed with between 1,000 and 1,500 soldiers. Electrical power is provided by a couple of Paul Bunyan-sized generators located outside. The backstage area is stocked with rolls and cold cuts and a tub with ice and bottled water and sodas. I dig into it like a man who doesn't care that he just watched raw sewage pouring over his bedroom floor.

The show itself is a comedian's dream come true. There is a mutual appreciation that you just don't get stateside. Even when I'm picking on soldiers in the audience they know I have nothing but respect and admiration for what they are doing. Most of the laughs I get come from how little I know about the military. My act is about laughing with people, not at them.

Joey and I both receive a military coin and thanks from an impressive colonel who reminds me of a young Sidney Poitier. I have no doubt he will be a future senator. They set up a table where Joey and I sign some autographs and take pictures. The exhaustion we felt earlier has been replaced with the adrenalin pump that comes with a great show.

Our evening was not over yet.

While I was doing my set, Joey learned about a hospital tent on base, where there were some guys that could not make the show. So, we'll take the show to them.

The hospital tent is pitched near the runway at the airport. It is dark, and as we step out of our vehicles, an F16 roars up the runway and takes off almost vertically. It is amazing. I've always heard that people like to see the Space Shuttle take off at night. Now I know why.

The tent was desert tan. I tilted my head as we entered, because the ceiling hung low in spots. We met the staff, and had a short discussion about which patients we would see. I was nervous. I did not know exactly what I was going to see or how I would react.

I had done hospital shows for people in New York City when I lived there, but this felt different. We met soldiers lying in beds, each with different injuries, some of them fresh. Joey and I made small talk and joked a bit, and I wished I was more famous. These guys deserve an A-list celebrity, maybe a sponge bath from Pamela Anderson.

Then it's show time. In a different part of the tent, they had set up about twenty chairs. It took some time to round up our crowd, soldiers in various stages of recovery. Some had been injured earlier that day. As Joey does his set, members of the staff wander in and stand in the back of the room. There are about thirty people in the area, some of them pretty banged up, but the laughter fills the room. As I watch, I think about the injured soldiers and the miraculous job done by the doctors and nurses, and am over-whelmed. We had just performed for 1,500 in a large theater, but this is a whole new experience. Joey finishes his set and I go up to do mine, and as I go into my act can feel myself getting choked up onstage. I don't want anyone to know, so do about twenty minutes and close the show out.

Joey and I make the rounds and take some pictures. As we

leave, a doctor follows us out of the tent. We stand on a quiet run-way, in the dark.

"That was great," he says. "It's the first time I've heard some of these guys laugh."

Chapter Forty Four

Jim McCue at Abu Ghraib prison.

We skip breakfast to sleep late, until 8 a.m. We grab some cappuccino on our way to the helipad, where a Black Hawk picks us up. Airborne, we absently watch the terrain below.

We begin circling a compound, and can see the men in orange jump suits. As we ready our descent, I realize that I've seen this place before.

We never receive an advance itinerary, but this is still a total surprise. It is the most recognizable stop on the trip, thanks to the avalanche of negative press about the place. As we scurry from the Black Hawk to a couple of waiting vans, someone from our welcoming committee sticks a hand out and offers a firm handshake.

"Welcome to Abu Ghraib Prison."

This immediately jumps to the top of my list of strange places to hold standup comedy shows. The first thing we're told -- ironically, I think -- is that we can't take pictures. There is no one on a leash or anything, but I can understand how the soldiers might be a little sensitive.

We are given a tour of the prison.

The prisoners all appear healthy, I note, as we make our way to the death house. Outside is the courtyard where it is said that thousands of people were sentenced to death under the Hussein regime. One of the soldiers tells us that when the court got backed up Saddam or one of his kids would come down and shoot every third person in line. I wonder if Saddam will have the same concern for speedy justice when they put him on trial.

Not surprisingly, the death house is a creepy place. As we enter, we pass an indoor gallows, where the previous regime had switched from using rope to using wire, because the ropes kept wearing out. Most of the apparatus is built of concrete, and even a yeoman like me can see how efficient the operation was. A ramp leads to an area under the hatches, designed to make it easy to push a wheel barrel in and out to fetch human remains.

Up the hallway are small cells where Saddam's prisoners were beaten and tortured. We can see, on the inside of the cells, where prisoners wrote their names in their own blood in hopes that their families would know what happened to them.

When we get back to the courtyard, it feels good to be back out in the fresh air and sunlight, like waking from a nightmare.

We return to the vans and head to our performance space. This afternoon's show will be held indoors in a hardened facility, which a soldier tells me will protect us from mortar attack.

"Yeah," I say, "but not from me bombing."

This will be a "by invitation only" performance, and for security reasons, none of the Iraqi nationals that work on base are allowed in. There will be soldiers posted at the door.

The soldiers have hamburgers and hotdogs, boxes of chips and tub filled with cold sodas and bottled water. It is our first Baghdad barbeque. There are soldiers on stage playing instruments, reminding me of a garage band. They are pretty good, but more to the point, they seem to be having a good time. I don't imagine they find much time for rehearsal.

About 500 soldiers pack the benches of the facility, and

really enjoy seeing their fellow soldiers perform. The show seems to start officially when the guitarist plays a respectable Jimi Hendrix version of the "Star Spangled Banner" on the electric guitar. It is Joey's turn to open, then me, and the crowd is great.

Before we arrived here, there was an incident of a female soldier mud wrestling and having her top pulled off in the process. As a result she was reprimanded. I made the observation that if we are punishing our females for topless mud wrestling, the terrorists have already won.

I don't know if that joke will ever get as good a response as it did that day.

Afterwards, Joey and I do an interview for Stars and Stripes, the military newspaper. We never read the interview, but somewhere it's documented that I was once the headliner at Abu Ghraib prison.

Chapter Forty Five

Marines in Falujah

We sign some autographs, shake some hands, and are back on the Black Hawk by 3 p.m. How do you top an afternoon show at Abu Ghraib? You do the next show in Fallujah.

Located forty miles west of Baghdad, Fallujah had been one of the most violent areas in Iraq until just a few months ago. That was when many of the marines we will soon be entertaining won one of the key battles for Iraq.

I like marines. My dad is a former marine and I think the marine influence on my dad contributed to the emotional scarring that produces a good comedian.

We take a short tour of the base and meet several marines, including some from a psychological warfare unit. I'm sure it must be a unit in which my girlfriend has trained.

We were in the company of a sergeant major whose polite swagger and confidence made me feel this really was "his" base.

While touring the base we hear some stories about how the insurgents would use civilians by shooting them and pushing them into the street to slow the marines' advance. The insurgents knew our soldiers would slow down to give these people medical aid.

We grabbed a bite at the dining facility, where a marine captain stood up and told everyone to pipe down. You could hear a pin drop. He then barked out an invitation to our show tonight and told the marines to enjoy their lunch. "Ooo rah," they grunted in unison, which I believe is the way marines RSVP.

We head to the theater where our gear is being stored. It is growing dark and there is another spectacular Irag sunset. By the time we return from the showers it is pitch black.

We are pulling on our clothes in the dressing room, when a three-star Marine Corps general walks in to the theater and addresses our audience. Even the plants stand at attention when this guy enters. His name is Gen. Michael W. Hagee , and the talk he gives is exceptionally powerful. He talks about the fact that they had been though a lot in the battle of Fallujah and how one marine in particular performed with exceptional valor. He also tells them that it is OK to laugh and that tonight is a night for laughter and joy. Then he brings me up and we are off and running. The show is great, and the general is sitting front and center, laughing the loudest.

After the show I ask him for a picture. He seems a little reluctant until I tell him my dad is a former marine.

He smiles and says, "You got me then."

After the show, a few marines invite me to share a victory cigar. Because alcohol is off limits, the offer of a good cigar with a coffee, instead of brandy, sounds pretty good. I don't usually smoke cigars unless it's a special occasion, but just being in the company of these guys rates this as an occasion I will not soon forget.

We walk back to the sergeant major's office. He has a small home theater he has constructed in a tool-shed sized metallic shipping container. He asks if we would like to watch a movie. To our amazement, he puts on a DVD of comedian Pablo Francisco. Pablo Francisco is a great comedian, but the last thing Joey and I want to do is watch a DVD of stand-up comedy. The sergeant major picks up on our lack of enthusiasm and asks what we want to see. I say jokingly,

"How about something about tourism in Fallujah."

"How about some tape we shot during the battle of Fallujah?"

"Hell, yes."

On the video, we got a play-by-play of the events and some history of the insurgency in the area. It was interesting, but only lasted about 10 minutes before a soldier came in and announced that our chopper was inbound. Within minutes we were back in the air. It was our first night flight.

The helicopters used by the USMC are larger and banana shaped. I only know the type called a Chinook, which sounds to me like a guy who sleeps with his sled dog. Anyway, the inside of this helicopter has room for a lot more men and cargo.

There are two gunners facing our in either direction manning fifty-caliber machine guns. They are both wearing night vision equipment. I think back to the night vision goggles that we tried at the start of our tour, back in Kosovo. I remember wondering how well these guys could see the ground. Our view is not nearly as good of the ground as it was in the Black Hawks, but I figured the bad guys would not have nearly as good a view of us and that was fine by me.

Chapter Forty Six

Tanks -a-lot for Ramadi

A day that had started at Anaconda and continued through the Abu Ghraib prison and a marine base in Fallujah would soon end in Ramadi, seventy miles west of Baghdad on the Euphrates River.

It is dark and I am punchy when we arrive. We are brought to a brick and mortar building that has sand bags covering the windows and stacked bunker style around the exits and entrances. We learn that there has been some kind of snafu regarding our sleeping quarters.

As we wait for them to straighten out the arrangements, I go outside with a marine major who has accompanied us from Fallujah. He lets me borrow his satellite phone and I try to make a few calls, but can reach no one.

It is just as well, because due to security concerns the conversation would have probably gone something like, "I'm still in Iraq … can't tell you where. How about those Red Sox?"

Because of the late hour, it is decided that the best sleeping arrangement is to set up some cots in a small recreation room in the bunker/building. There is a female officer who'd joined our party; she'd sleep in a different part of the building.

Frankly, and I mean this in a complimentary way, I think this officer would have been fine if they told her she needed to sleep outdoors, standing up, in a sand storm. The females in the military, especially the Marine Corps, carry their own weight.

Thankfully, comedians are held to a lesser standard. I have some trouble setting up my cot because I'm about as handy as a Phillips head screwdriver when you need a cup of coffee, but get it set up, wash up, and hit the hay. I fall asleep as soon as my head hits the spot where a pillow should be. It might as well be a king-sized bed, even though my feet are dangling about eight inches off the end.

At one point, I wake up to go to the latrine, and I remember the story of a soldier who got killed in the latrine by a mortar. I shudder, and hustle back to my safe, almost comfortable cot.

The next morning, on the way back from the showers, I run into the officer and private who had traveled with us from Fallujah. They are headed to the PX, and I accompany them, hoping to find something for my girlfriend or perhaps locate the elusive Harley T-shirt for my brother-in-law. For some reason, there was a line of about 100 soldiers, who were being allowed in two at a time as other people exited the store.

Some soldiers passed the time by playing a game where you put your hand down on a flat surface. You open your fingers and see how fast you can take a knife and stick the wood in between the spaces of your fingers without stabbing yourself. This is not a game for piano players. Every once in awhile, you would hear somebody miss.

"Ouch."

"Shit."

Laughter, followed by, "Okay... Your turn."

It is a game I can only imagine young men playing. I just can't envision young women sitting around saying, "You know what would be fun? Let's get some darts and throw them at each other."

The wait at the PX was about thirty minutes, and when we got in I found nothing for Bernadette and no Harley T-shirt. I was starting to think I was going to strike out.

We all went back to the building and gathered our group for breakfast. Our host in Ramadi was Sgt. Ahern from Lowell, Massachusetts. He, Joey and I compared notes from our prospective New England upbringings. He gave Joey and me two light jackets with the unit insignia. I was delighted when both jackets turned out to be XXL and fit only me. Joey muttered something and gave me his jacket. Joey and I used to be roommates and it was kind of a running gag that every time I shrunk something, Joey got a new sweater.

After breakfast we took a tour of the base, which included an introduction to the M1A1 tank, which has a jet turbine engine. To me, it sounds like something designed by a red neck engineer.

"Bring in that tank and an F16. I got me an idea."

If it was designed by a red neck engineer, you know it will only be a matter of time before it shows up on the NASCAR circuit.

I don't know if we'll ever see it on the race track, but what I'd really like to do is drive it out on the highway with those Boston drivers. I don't think those SUVs would crowd me quite as much as they do in my car.

Our next stop is to meet with a small weapons expert. He shows us with a great deal of pride many of the weapons that we have seized from the insurgents. I hope we are able to take a hell of a lot more guns away from the insurgents.

At 2 p.m., we go to the MWR facility and do a show. It is a lot of fun, and after the show and the autographs we go to get a bite to eat. After eating, we are standing outside the dining facility when we hear four loud explosions. I look to Sgt. Ahern.

"Incoming," he says.

As the words come out of his mouth, the siren sounds. It is like something I've seen and heard in movies. People begin hustling to bunkers and into buildings.

Ahern is calm.

"Do you want to run for a bunker?"

"You've been here for a year," I say. "If you say 'Shit,' that's what I'll do."

We all laugh, nervously.

"By the time you hear the explosions or the sirens, the attack is usually over," Ahern says. "That's the nature of the insurgents' attack -- hit and run. They don't even aim; they just lob the mortars and hope to get lucky."

He is right. There are no more explosions, and we have a chopper to catch. Later, Joey will tell me that when he returned to pick up some gear from the building we stayed at last night, he could smell sulfur in the air.

I recall my trip to the latrine last night, and think that sometimes timing is everything.

It is cold and dark as we wait at the airfield, and I fish through my luggage and pull out the two jackets given to us by Sgt. Ahern. Joey and I bundle up as the lieutenant colonel uses a flashlight to fish out some power bars. We can hear the hydraulics of tanks and artillery acquiring a target. After a few minutes, the machines fall silent without firing. Maybe the targets were too near a mosque or school or something.

We don't have much time to dwell on that question, because our Chinooks are landing and it is time for my second night flight in a marine helicopter.

Chapter Forty Seven

Marines enjoying the show at FOB Tauquddum

After about a two and a half hour flight we arrive at FOB Tau-quddum, (TQ for short) at 7:35 p.m. We are driven to our quarters, two rooms with two single beds and one bathroom. I clean up first and head over to check out where we will be performing. The base seems pretty big to me.

There is a huge stage outdoors, with folding chairs set up in front of it. It is cold and raw, and I notice that when Joey shows up he is still wearing the over-sized jacket I loaned him earlier. At this point you might ask yourself who in their right mind would sit outside in the cold at night in the middle of Iraq to watch two comedians.

The marines, of course.

Our finale in Iraq is great. The marines fill the seats and stand in the back or sit on large mounds of earth piled up about 40 or 50 yards from the stage. Joey goes up and does a great job -- even though a chopper comes in during the set and then an ambulance cuts through our audience. The chopper obviously makes a lot of noise, but the true disturbance is the ambulance, which brings a reverent hush as it quietly drives through the crowd.

It is Joey's job, on stage, to break the tension.

"Well," he says. "I know the show's going bad when they send an ambulance for me."

We close out the show, and afterwards sit at a table signing autographs and shaking the hands of these brave servicemen and woman. It is bittersweet, but it is time to return home. It is time to return to family and friends and clean underwear, indoor plumbing and my own bed. I look around and hope that everyone here will be home soon.

Chapter Forty Eight

Jim McCue captures Iraq plane but can't afford to fly it home.

The next day, we take a quick tour of TQ, including a field littered with downed bombers. We take pictures and wonder about the sequence of events that brought them to this place. We walk around and can see these aircraft riddled with bullet holes. At one point I climbed up on a crate to get my picture taken on the wing. I was lucky to make it off without breaking my neck. Joey, ever wanting to one-up me in the high functioning dumb-ass contest, decides to climb into a tail gunner turret to get his picture taken. I try to talk him out of it.

We had seen pictures of a critter called a camel spider, which is about the nastiest little beast you have ever seen. Now, for some reason, I am picturing a nest of camel spiders waiting for some dumb ass to climb in for a picture in one of these abandoned aircraft. I keep telling Joey I think it is a bad idea, but he doesn't listen.

Well, to make a short story long, Joey climbs in, gets his picture taken and nothing happens. There are no camel spiders, no scorpions, not even a Middle Eastern mosquito.

So, I jump in right after him, and have my picture taken. It might seem reckless, but I had a good reason.

Monkey see, monkey do.

Chapter Forty Nine

Joey Carroll, Bobby Kelly, & Jim McCue

Our final stop in Iraq is at the airport. We are processed through security, and as we wait our party is joined by about fifty or so marines. They are traveling with us to Kuwait, and hopefully back home.

Proving that marines really can sleep anywhere, many of them sprawl out on the concrete floor and catch some Zs. An hour later, we are boarding a C-130, very similar to the airport that took us into this country.

Soldiers load the baggage and freight and us. The hydraulic ramp lifts to close the rear of the plane and we are bound for Kuwait. We are still in a steep climb when we hear a loud explosion. Through my small, porthole-shaped window, I see a bright ball of fire.

Later, Lt. Col. Saunders explains that the pilot shot off the plane's "counter measures." That means, in this case, he released a ball of fire with metallic confetti intended to draw a heat-seeking rocket away from the aircraft. In other words, someone shot a rocket at our plane.

Right now, inside the plane, it's too loud for explanations. I yell into Joey's ear "You have got to be shitting me."

Lt. Col. Saunders is across from me, and he's calm. Sure, I think, he didn't see the ball of fire. Anyway, nobody else is disturbed, and nothing else happens. I say a quiet prayer of thanks.

A few hours later we land in Kuwait. While collecting our things, we discover that two of our friends have been entertaining at bases during the Iraq leg of our tour as well, and were on the same plane that we were. Comedians Robert "Bobby" Kelly and Colin Quinn were sitting in the cockpit, and Bobby says that the enemy really did shoot something at the plane.

Chapter Fifty

Creepy Mural of Saddam with young girl in Uday's palace.

I'm often asked what I think of what is going on in Iraq. I don't know if I'm the best person to consult on national policy. I'm a freaking comedian. I do know that they just had an election where a record number of people took the risk to show up and vote. In the U.S.A., a lot of us don't vote if it rains. I think our military is the best in the world. I think that a lot of people will debate who knew what when it comes to WMD's. I believed that Saddam Hussein had them or was trying to acquire them. I think he was in violation of a boatload of United Nation resolutions and a lot of folks like French President Jacques Chirac and U.N. Secretary General Kofi Annan are looking like they were caught with their hands in the cookie jar. I think the number one thing we fear in the U.S.A. are weapons of mass destruction in the hands of terrorists. I think the number one thing feared by the mullahs and by dictators is freedom and democracy. I think we need to stop second-guessing our military. You cannot support the troops yet be against everything they try to accomplish. We are going to be in Iraq for a while, but there is no one I talked to who wants us to stay there. We want to get the Iraqi people in a place were they can support themselves and then pull out.

Entertaining our troops is the most rewarding thing I do. I sincerely do get more out of it then they do. I would urge anyone reading this to find a way to show support for our people in uniform. I went to Google and there are still bunches of ways you can support the troops. Just go on any search engine type in support of the troops and find a program that you believe will do the most good.

I have already gone to Germany and hosted my sixth annual battle of the army bands which is a competition run by some great people in Germany like Jim Shore who give soldiers the opportunity to compete and show off their musical talents.

Since I went on this tour I have a new appreciation for what is important. I don't complain as much about where I work. I appreciate that I live in a country where I can make fun of the president. I thank God for a president who is so easy to make fun of. I'm thankful for a hot shower and a warm bed. I have asked my girlfriend to marry me and she said yes. I love my family and friends. As I finish this book I am scheduled to return to Iraq for another tour. I look forward to all the great shows and people I will meet. I am a little scared. I look forward to returning home to enjoy all the freedoms that we have because of the sacrifices made by our men and woman in uniform.

When you say you support the troops, ask yourself how. If you want a better way to support them, go to the website www.anysoldier.org, the home of an organization that takes care of soldiers in need. Or do something even simpler. The next time you see someone in uniform, thank them for serving our country.

Trust me. Showing simple appreciation for the sacrifices they make goes a long way with soldiers, and it's free.

Thanks

I would like to thank God for getting me home safely and for my many blessings. I would like to thank my friends and family for all the support they have given me over the years. I would like to thank everyone who has ever given me a gig even the bad ones. I would like to thank AKA productions for booking me on this tour. I would also like to thank Mike Smith and Claire Presthus for proof reading this book. Last but never least I would like to thank the brave men and women who serve in the US military.

Here is a list of people whom I would like to thank.

God
The U.S. military & their families
AKA Productions
Our family & friends
Barbara Rattigan
MWR
Allen "MAC" McNeil
"Road Rage" Rudy
Dwayne Ulloa
Casey Cmiel
Lt. Col. Eddie "King of the Hill" Saunders
Col. Glass
Sgt. Sharp
Airman Carmen
Sgt. Ahern
Jim Sohre
Capt. Zimmerman
Capt. Elizabeth Condon
General Sullivan
General Sattler
Col. Vicci
Michael Yon
Capt. Hermesch
Donnie from MWR
Mrs. Bernadette McCue
Anyone else I missed...sorry, it was a long trip!
Historical information obtained from globalsecurity.org